MIRANDA v. ARIZONA

ABDO
Publishing Company

Landmark Supreme Court Cases

MIRANDA v. ARIZONA

AN INDIVIDUAL'S RIGHTS WHEN UNDER ARREST

by Sue Vander Hook

Content Consultant

Yale Kamisar, Clarence Darrow Distinguished University Professor Emeritus of Law,
University of Michigan

CREDITS

Published by ABDO Publishing Company, PO Box 398166, Minneapolis, MN 55439. Copyright © 2013 by Abdo Consulting Group, Inc. International copyrights reserved in all countries. No part of this book may be reproduced in any form without written permission from the publisher. The Essential Library™ is a trademark and logo of ABDO Publishing Company.

Printed in the United States of America, North Mankato, Minnesota
042012
092012

 THIS BOOK CONTAINS AT LEAST 10% RECYCLED MATERIALS.

Editor: Lauren Coss
Series Designer: Emily Love

Library of Congress Cataloging-in-Publication Data
Vander Hook, Sue, 1949-
  Miranda v. Arizona : an individual's rights when under arrest / By Sue Vander Hook ; content consultant Yale Kamisar.
    p. cm. -- (Landmark Supreme Court cases)
  Includes bibliographical references.
  ISBN 978-1-61783-474-5
  1. Miranda, Ernesto--Trials, litigation, etc.--Juvenile literature. 2. Trials (Rape)--Arizona--Juvenile literature. 3. Self-incrimination--United States--Juvenile literature. 4. Right to counsel--United States--Juvenile literature. 5. Police questioning--United States--Juvenile literature. 6. Trial and arbitral proceedings I. Kamisar, Yale. II. Title. III. Title: Miranda vs. Arizona. IV. Title: Miranda versus Arizona.
  KF224.M54V38 2013
  345.73'056--dc23

                              2012001278

Photo Credits
Jack Dagley Photography/Shutterstock Images, cover, 129; AP Images, 9, 28, 35, 71, 108, 114, 117; Robert Houston/AP Images, 18; Library of Congress, 21; National Archives, 24; Bettmann/Corbis/AP Images, 30, 62, 88, 101, 120; Arizona State Library, Archives and Public Records, History and Archives Division, 3, 39, 47, 48; Harris & Ewing/Library of Congress, 66; Gary Blakeley/Shutterstock Images, 79; Henry Burroughs/AP Images, 112; Alan Singer/NBCU Photo Bank/Getty Images, 131; Missouri Department of Corrections/AP Images, 135; MPI/Getty Images, 137

Table of Contents

WHAT IS THE US SUPREME COURT?

The US Supreme Court, located in Washington DC, is the highest court in the United States and authorized to exist by the US Constitution. It consists of a chief justice and eight associate justices nominated by the president of the United States and approved by the US Senate. The justices are appointed to serve for life. A term of the court is from the first Monday in October to the first Monday in October the following year.

Each year, the justices are asked to consider more than 7,000 cases. They vote on which petitions they will grant. Four of the nine justices must vote in favor of granting a petition before a case moves forward. Currently, the justices decide between 100 and 150 cases per term.

The justices generally choose cases that address questions of state or federal laws or other constitutional questions they have not previously ruled on. The Supreme Court cannot simply declare a law unconstitutional; it must wait until someone appeals a lower court's ruling on the law.

HOW DOES THE APPEALS PROCESS WORK?

A case usually begins in a local court. For a case involving a federal law, this is usually a federal district court. For a case involving a state or local law, this is a local trial court.

If a defendant is found guilty in a criminal trial and believes the trial court made an error, that person may appeal the case to a higher court. The defendant, now called an appellant, files a brief that explains the error the trial court allegedly made and asks for the decision to be reversed.

An appellate court, or court of appeals, reviews the records of the lower court but does not look at other evidence or call witnesses. If the appeals court finds no errors were made, the appellant may go one step further and petition the US Supreme Court to review the case. A case ruled on in a state's highest court may be appealed to the US Supreme Court.

A Supreme Court decision is based on a majority vote. Occasionally one or more justices will abstain from a case, however, a majority vote by the remaining justices is still needed to overturn a lower-court ruling. What the US Supreme Court decides is final; there is no other court to which a person can appeal. In addition, these rulings set precedent for future rulings. Unless the circumstances are greatly changed, the Supreme Court makes rulings that are consistent with its past decisions. Only an amendment to the US Constitution can overturn a Supreme Court ruling.

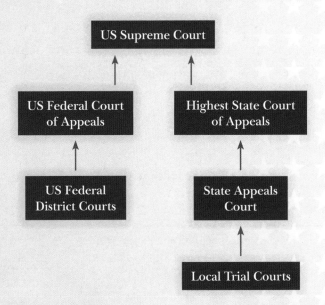

Chapter 1

Waiting for an Answer

In the summer of 1965, Ernesto Miranda was serving time in the Arizona State Prison in Florence, Arizona. The prison's mission-style Spanish architecture, red tile roof, and twin palm trees in front disguised the harsh interior. Inside, small cells housed the most dangerous criminals in the state. Some inmates were on death row, waiting for the day when they would be executed by lethal injection or in the gas chamber. Other inmates hoped for early parole; several waited for their **sentences** to be up. Miranda

---

sentence—A decision by a judge or court including the punishment for the person convicted.

Ernesto Miranda had no idea the effect his appeal to the Supreme Court would have on the future of law enforcement.

was waiting to learn if the United States Supreme Court, the highest court in the country, would agree to hear his case. This was his last chance and his last hope to get out of prison.

Cut-and-Dried Case?

Miranda had already served two years of his 20- to 30-year prison sentence for kidnapping and rape. In June 1963, his trial had been held in the Superior Court of Maricopa County, Arizona, which hears criminal cases such as murder and rape. Alvin Moore, Miranda's court-appointed attorney, did his best to get an **acquittal** for his client. But the victim's **testimony**, the physical evidence, and Miranda's written confession made it a cut-and-dried case.

After the trial, Moore **appealed** his client's **conviction** to the Arizona Supreme Court, the highest court in the state. In his appeal, Moore claimed Miranda had not been given a fair trial and listed several errors the trial court had made. It was up to the **appellate court** to determine if errors had, in fact, occurred. The court would not decide if Miranda was guilty or innocent, but it would decide whether he had received a fair trial. If the appellate court found Miranda had not received a fair trial, his case would be returned to the Superior Court of Maricopa County, where Miranda would be tried again for the same crimes.

Moore believed the trial court made an error by entering Miranda's confession into evidence. Moore argued that the confession had not been received in a fair way. He asked the appellate court, "Was [Miranda's] statement made voluntarily?"[1] He asked the court another question, "Was [Miranda] (a Mexican boy of limited education) afforded all the safeguards to his rights provided by the Constitution of the United States and the law and rules of the courts?"[2] Moore also brought up the testimony of the rape victim. At that time, Arizona state **prosecutors** had to prove a rape victim had "resist[ed] to the utmost."[3] Moore claimed the prosecutor had not proved this fact.

acquittal—A verdict that frees a criminal suspect from charges.

appealed—Petitioned a higher court to review the decision or proceedings of a lower court.

appellate court—A court that can review and reverse the judgment of a lower court.

conviction—The process of finding someone guilty.

prosecutor—A lawyer who brings legal action against someone.

testimony—Something declared in court under oath.

Right to an Attorney

Moore's appeal claimed that Miranda was never informed of his right to have a lawyer present during his police interrogation. His confession, therefore, should not have been admitted into evidence at trial. According to Carroll Cooley, lead investigating officer, Miranda confessed to the crimes voluntarily without being threatened or coerced. Cooley said Miranda not only admitted "he was the person that had raped this girl," but he also admitted he tried to rape another woman and rob yet another.[4] Miranda then agreed to write down how he had raped the 18-year-old woman.

Miranda's confession described how he told the young woman to take off her clothes. She refused to do so and asked him to take her home. He admitted to taking off the woman's clothes, raping her, and telling her to get her clothes back on. His written confession ended with these words:

> " Seen a girl walking up street stopped a little ahead of her got out of car walked towards her grabbed her by the arm and asked to get in the car. Got in car without force tied hands & ankles. Drove away for a few miles."[5]
>
> —ERNESTO MIRANDA

"Drove her home. I couldn't say I was sorry for what I had done. But asked her to say a prayer for me."[6] At the trial, Miranda's confession was entered into evidence and used to convict him.

At the original trial, Cooley testified he had informed Miranda of his **constitutional** rights. When Cooley was on the witness stand, Defense Attorney Moore asked him, "Did you warn [Miranda] of his rights?"[7] Cooley answered, "Yes, sir, at the heading of the statement is a paragraph typed out, and I read this paragraph to him out loud."[8] The paragraph read,

> *I, Ernest A. Miranda, do hereby swear that I make this statement voluntarily and out of my own free will, with no threats, coercion, or promises of immunity, and with full knowledge of my legal rights, understanding any statement I make may be used against me.*[9]

Moore continued his questioning: "But did you ever, before or during your conversation or before taking this statement, did you ever advise the defendant he was entitled to the services of an attorney?"[10]

---

constitutional—In accordance with a constitution.

Cooley responded that Miranda's rights were included in the statement read to him. But Moore challenged Cooley further, "I don't see in the statement that it says where he is entitled to the advise [sic] of an attorney before he made it."[11] "No sir," answered Cooley. "It doesn't say anything about an attorney."[12] Cooley admitted he never informed Miranda of his right to have the assistance of a lawyer. Later, Cooley stated Miranda "was not unknowledgeable about his rights. He was an ex-convict . . . and had been through the routine before."[13] Cooley believed Miranda already knew about his right to an attorney since he had been arrested before.

Appeal Denied

On April 22, 1965, the Arizona Supreme Court ruled no errors were made at the original trial. The court unanimously denied Miranda's appeal and affirmed the trial court's conviction. The Arizona Supreme Court's justices stated that a "confession may be admissible when made without an attorney if it is voluntary and does not violate constitutional rights of **defendant**."[14] Because Miranda had been arrested several times before, the court ruled he was "familiar with legal proceedings and personal rights in court."[15] Therefore, he already knew what his constitutional rights were.

THE SIXTH AMENDMENT

The Sixth Amendment to the US Constitution protects the rights of the accused in a criminal proceeding. This includes the right to a speedy trial, the right to a public trial, and the right to an unbiased jury. Defendants must also be informed of the accusations against them. Defendants are allowed to confront or question any witnesses against them as well as obtain witnesses of their own. The amendment concludes with the right of the accused to have an attorney who will assist him or her in defense.

Moore, however, was still convinced police investigators should have told Miranda about his right to an attorney. He believed the court had denied Miranda the rights guaranteed every US citizen under the Sixth Amendment to the Constitution of the United States. The Sixth Amendment had been in force since 1791, when the Bill of Rights became the first ten amendments to the Constitution. The Sixth Amendment clearly states: "the accused shall enjoy the right to . . . have the Assistance of Counsel for his defense."[16] But two courts had now ruled Miranda had not been denied his rights under the Sixth Amendment. Miranda had only one

defendant—The person against whom legal action is brought.

more chance to convince a court his constitutional rights had been violated. He would have to file a petition for a **writ of certiorari** with the Supreme Court of the United States.

Petition to the US Supreme Court

Seventy-five-year-old Moore did not want to represent Miranda in another appeal, so Miranda wrote the petition to the US Supreme Court himself. He mailed his petition to the court early in June 1965. Miranda's petition was one of more than 1,000 others the court received that term. Lawyers filed petitions with eloquent words neatly typed on watermarked paper. But hundreds of prisoners filed petitions on their own behalf. These were usually handwritten in pencil or crayon on cheap paper. Those prisoners hoped the justices would notice their petitions and review their cases.

Letter from the Court

Once Miranda submitted his petition, all he could do was wait. At least four US Supreme Court justices

writ of certiorari—An order from a higher court to a lower court calling for the record of a case for review.

THE AMERICAN CIVIL LIBERTIES UNION

The American Civil Liberties Union (ACLU) exists to fight for the civil rights of Americans, even if the cause is unpopular. A small group of people concerned with protecting civil rights founded the ACLU in 1920. Since then, it has expanded to include 500,000 members and supporters. Its staff and volunteer lawyers handle civil liberties cases across the country. They often handle cases involving groups of people who have been denied their rights, including homosexual people, people with disabilities, and prisoners, such as Miranda.

had to grant his petition and agree to review his trial proceedings and first appeal. He did not have to wait very long. On June 18, 1965, just weeks after submitting his petition, Miranda received an envelope from the clerk of the US Supreme Court. The envelope contained Miranda's petition for a writ of certiorari, returned to him—unread—because of an error in his submission. His petition had never made it to the private meeting of the justices.

Miranda's hopes were dashed. But little did he know that just three days earlier, Robert J. Corcoran, a volunteer at the American Civil Liberties Union (ACLU) in Phoenix, Arizona, had read about Miranda's case. It caught Corcoran's attention because it was about

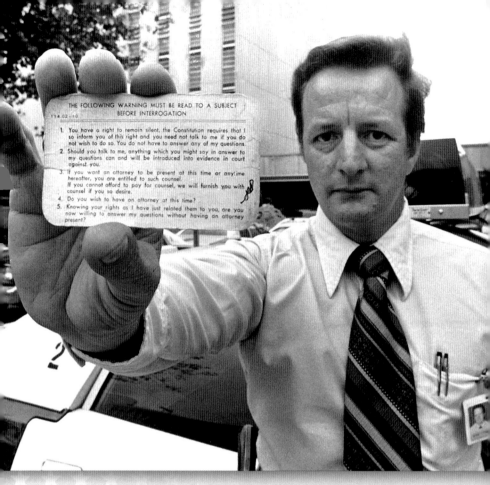

A law enforcement official holds up a Miranda warning card. Miranda's appeal was based on the violation of several constitutional rights, which are discussed on the card.

the rights of the accused. As a former deputy county attorney, Corcoran often interrogated suspects in criminal cases. He was very careful to inform the accused of "the right to remain silent, the right to the assistance of an attorney, and the fact that anything said could be used against him or her."[17] He had never had a case overturned on appeal for not informing a suspect of his or her rights.

Corcoran believed that protecting a person's constitutional rights was so important, it was time for the US Supreme Court to consider it. Corcoran wrote a letter to Moore and asked for his help in filing a petition with the US Supreme Court. Moore declined, but Corcoran made sure a petition was filed with the court anyway. The ensuing case would change the meaning of Miranda from a person's name to a term that would forever be associated with a person's constitutional rights. ～

Chapter 2

Rights of the Accused

In 1789, the United States of America was a very new nation. Representatives from each of the 13 states were in heated debate over the new constitution. Some states refused to ratify it unless a list of basic individual rights was included. James Madison, a congressman of Virginia, took on the task of drafting what would become the Bill of Rights. He included freedom of speech, freedom of the press, the right to keep and bear arms, and the right to a trial by **jury**.

jury—A group of people selected to deliver a verdict on an issue, such as a court case.

James Madison laid out personal freedoms for US citizens
with the Bill of Rights.

Madison also included protection for citizens accused of a crime. The accused could not be forced to make self-incriminating statements. In addition, the accused was guaranteed the right to a speedy trial and the right to legal counsel. However, this protection of rights applied only to defendants being tried for federal offenses or **capital crimes**.

The Bill of Rights was added to the US Constitution on December 15, 1791, as the first ten amendments. These pertained to the federal government, not the states' governments. It did not apply to people accused of crimes violating state laws such as murder, rape, and armed robbery. Each US state and the District of Columbia had its own constitution and legal procedures for those crimes.

INSISTING ON A BILL OF RIGHTS

In 1787, delegates from the 13 states met to draft the Constitution of the United States. Over the next four years, intense debates raged because the Constitution did not include a list of individual rights. Thomas Jefferson, who drafted the Declaration of Independence, argued in a letter to James Madison, "A bill of rights is what the people are entitled to against every government on earth."[1]

Questionable Interrogation Techniques

At that time, only a few states granted their citizens the right to be represented by counsel. Police had few restrictions. Confessions were obtained through "beatings, pistol whippings . . . solitary confinement in rat-infested jail cells, [and] application of the 'water cure'—holding a suspect's head under water for long periods" of time.[2] Forced confessions usually resulted in guilty verdicts. Some convicted defendants appealed their cases to the US Supreme Court, but the court was hesitant to interfere with state legal systems.

Constitutional Rights

It was not until the Fourteenth Amendment was passed on July 9, 1868, that courts considered whether the constitutional right of **due process of law** should apply to all states. The Fourteenth Amendment, enacted after the Civil War, primarily granted citizenship to former slaves, but it also forbids any state from denying any person "life, liberty or property, without due process of

capital crime—A crime that is punishable by death.

due process of law—A basic principle in the US legal system that requires fairness in the government's dealings with people.

The Constitution of the United States is the basis
for the country's laws and government.

law."[3] The amendment reinforces two other amendments
to the Constitution—the fifth and the sixth, which spell
out the rights of the accused.

The Fifth Amendment protects the accused from self-incrimination by saying anything that would prove his or her own guilt. It states in part, "nor shall [a person] be compelled in any criminal case to be a witness against himself, nor be deprived of life, liberty, or property, without due process of law."[4] The Sixth Amendment gives the accused even more rights:

> *In all criminal prosecutions, the accused shall enjoy the right to a speedy and public trial . . . and to be informed of the nature and cause of the accusation; to be confronted with the witnesses against him; to have compulsory process for obtaining witnesses in his favor, and to have the Assistance of Counsel for his defence [sic].*[6]

However, an accused's right to counsel was rather limited. Anyone who wanted a lawyer and could afford one was allowed the services of an attorney. But this left

PLEADING THE FIFTH

"Pleading the Fifth" is used by people who do not want to incriminate themselves. The expression refers to the Fifth Amendment to the Constitution, which states, "No person . . . shall be compelled in any criminal case to be a witness against himself."[5]

In 1929, President Herbert Hoover appointed a committee to study the history of crime and law enforcement in the United States. In 1931, the committee's findings were published in 14 volumes. One volume, *Lawlessness in Law Enforcement*, is a shocking revelation of police misconduct. It exposes widespread police brutality and the common practice of questioning a suspect to the "'third degree'—the willful infliction of pain and suffering on criminal suspects."[7] The report also reveals corruption in the criminal justice system, including "bribery, entrapment, coercion of witnesses, fabrication of evidence, and illegal wiretapping."[8]

out those who were not aware of that right and those who could not afford an attorney. It was not until the 1930s that the Supreme Court ruled on a case that gave every person charged with a federal offense the right to an attorney, regardless of a defendant's ability to pay. That right was first tested in 1932, in *Powell v. Alabama*.

Powell v. Alabama

In March 1931, nine illiterate African-American teenage men were onboard a freight train traveling through Alabama. Seven white teenage men and two young white women were also on the train. A fight developed between the two male groups; all but one of the white men was thrown off the train. When the train stopped, a sheriff's posse arrested the nine African-American men and took them into custody in Scottsboro, Alabama. The two white women then claimed they had been raped by six of the African-American men.

The trial judge ordered the Alabama State Bar, the organization charged with licensing and overseeing Alabama lawyers, to provide attorneys for the young men. However, no lawyers represented any of the teenagers until the day of the trial. The attorneys who went to court for the swift, one-day trials were unprepared and had not talked to the defendants before court convened. The trials ended in guilty verdicts and death sentences for eight of the nine men, who came to be known as the Scottsboro Boys.

The American Communist Party took up the case and provided an attorney to appeal to the Alabama State Supreme Court. This court upheld the convictions in a 6–1 decision. In the one **dissenting** vote, Chief Justice John C. Anderson strongly asserted that the defendants had not been given a fair trial.

dissent—An official written statement of a Supreme Court justice who disagrees with the majority decision.

Attorney Samuel Leibowitz, *center*, is shown with four of the Scottsboro Boys. The American Communist Party hired Leibowitz to represent the Scottsboro Boys.

A petition for a writ of certiorari was then filed with the US Supreme Court, arguing that the defendants had been denied their Fifth Amendment protection against self-incrimination, their right to counsel according to the Sixth Amendment, and due process of law according to the Fourteenth Amendment.

The petition went on to state that the right to counsel and "sufficient time to advise with counsel" is a fundamental right. The petition declared that if a defendant is incapable of defending himself "adequately because of ignorance, feeble-mindedness, illiteracy or the like, it is the duty of the court, whether requested or not, to assign counsel for him as a necessary requisite of due process of law."[9]

On November 7, 1932, the US Supreme Court ruled on *Powell vs. Alabama*, named after Ozie Powell, one of the Scottsboro Boys. The court ruled that the young men had been denied their constitutional rights. The Supreme Court reversed the lower court's convictions and ordered new trials for all the young men. It was the first time the US Supreme Court had reversed a lower court's decision because defendants had not been given their Fourteenth Amendment right of due process of law or their Sixth Amendment right to counsel. Supreme Court Justice George Sutherland wrote in his opinion,

After the Supreme Court ruling, Ozie Powell received a new trial in Decatur, Alabama, in 1933. This time a lawyer represented him.

We are of opinion that . . . the necessity of counsel was so vital and imperative that the failure of the trial court to make an effective appointment of counsel was likewise a denial of due process within the meaning of the Fourteenth Amendment.[10]

However, Sutherland made it clear that the right to appointed council in state cases was narrowly limited. He went on to address the illiteracy of the defendants:

[I]n a capital case, where the defendant is . . . incapable adequately of making his own defense because of ignorance, feeble mindedness, illiteracy, or the like, it is the duty of the court, whether requested or not, to assign counsel for him as a necessary requisite of due process of law.[11]

The *Powell* decision set the stage for other cases that would challenge the meaning of the Fifth, Sixth, and Fourteenth amendments.

Johnson v. Zerbst

In 1938, six years after *Powell*, the US Supreme Court reviewed *Johnson v. Zerbst*. Two men had been arrested and convicted of using counterfeit money—a federal offense. A lawyer did not represent the men at trial because they had no money, and the lower court did not provide a lawyer for them. The court claimed the defendants had automatically waived their rights to an attorney because they could not pay for one. On May 23, 1938, the US Supreme Court ruled federal defendants too poor to afford an attorney may have lawyers provided by the government.

The Supreme Court also ruled that a lower court must be absolutely sure a defendant has "competently and intelligently **waived** his constitutional right" to counsel. Otherwise, the defendant's Sixth Amendment rights have been violated.[12] The court stated,

> *The determination of whether there has been an intelligent waiver of right to counsel must depend, in each case, upon the particular facts and circumstances surrounding that case, including the background, experience, and conduct of the accused.*[13]

Powell and *Johnson* both laid a firm foundation for defendants to have the right to an attorney in federal cases. But the right to counsel had not yet been guaranteed to defendants on trial for state offenses.

Betts v. Brady

In 1942, four years after *Johnson*, a man, Betts, was arrested for robbery in the state of Maryland. The first time he appeared before the judge, Betts stated he wanted a lawyer but could not afford one. The judge denied his request and told Betts the county did not appoint lawyers for defendants who could not afford them except in cases of murder or rape. Betts represented himself at trial; he was found guilty and sentenced to eight years in prison. He appealed twice to state appellate courts, but those courts did not believe he had been denied his constitutional rights under the Fourteenth Amendment. As a last resort, Betts filed a petition for a writ of certiorari to the US Supreme Court.

The nation's highest court voted 6–3 that Betts did not have the right to an attorney since he was not tried in federal court. The **majority opinion** stated,

> *The Sixth Amendment of the national Constitution applies only to trials in federal courts. The due process clause of the Fourteenth Amendment does*

majority opinion—An explanation of the reasoning behind the majority decision of the Supreme Court.

waived—Willingly gave up.

not incorporate, as such, the specific guarantees found in the Sixth Amendment.[14]

The opinion also declared the state courts could decide on a case-by-case basis whether to provide an attorney to an impoverished defendant with insufficient funds to pay an attorney.

Gideon v. Wainwright

Betts delivered a hard blow to the Sixth Amendment, but the issue of the right to counsel was not over. More than 20 years later, on March 18, 1963, the Supreme Court overruled *Betts*. In *Gideon v. Wainwright*, defendant Clarence Earl Gideon, who had little money, was denied the right to counsel and defended himself at his trial for burglary. He was convicted and sentenced to prison. He eventually appealed his case to the US Supreme Court. After review and **oral arguments**, the nine justices agreed unanimously that state courts were required to provide an attorney for a defendant who could not afford one for any criminal case—not just federal or capital crimes.

oral argument—A spoken presentation of a legal case by a lawyer.

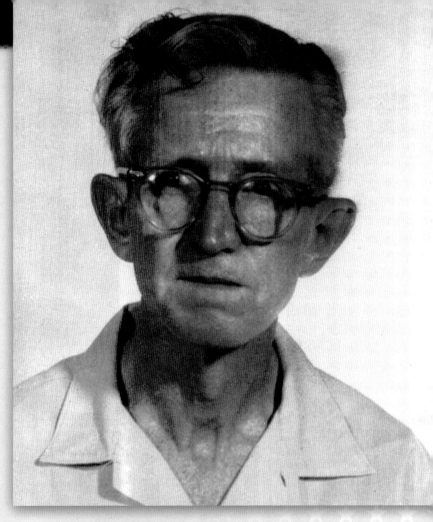

Clarence Earl Gideon, seen in 1963, was at the center of *Gideon v. Wainwright*, a critical case that preceded *Miranda*.

Gideon received a new trial; this time, an attorney represented him. He was acquitted and set free. The opinion of the Supreme Court stated clearly,

The right of [an impoverished] defendant in a criminal trial to have the assistance of counsel is a fundamental right essential to a fair trial, and petitioner's trial and conviction without the assistance of counsel violated the Fourteenth Amendment.[15]

The opinion stated the Sixth Amendment had no authority over the states, but it also emphasized that the right to counsel was so "fundamental and essential to a fair trial" that the states should be compelled to abide by it.[16]

> " Because the Due process clause of the fourteenth amendment of the Constitution and the fifth and sixth articles of the Bill of rights has been violated. . . . Petitioner receive Trial and sentence without aid of counsel, your petitioner was deprived 'Due process of law.' . . . Your petitioner was compelled to make his own defense, he was incapable adequately of making his own defense."[17]
>
> —CLARENCE EARL GIDEON, FROM HIS PETITION FOR A WRIT OF CERTIORARI IN 1962

Powell, Johnson, Betts, and *Gideon* were now the foundation for the Fifth, Sixth, and Fourteenth amendments. All US citizens had the right to be represented by an attorney even if they could not afford one. These

US Supreme Court cases set the stage for the trial and subsequent appeals of Ernesto Miranda, who was accused in 1963 of kidnapping and rape. The Supreme Court would once again become involved in deciding how broadly the Constitution could be interpreted when it came to the rights of the accused. ~

Chapter 3

The Man and His Crimes

In March 1963, the US Supreme Court ruled on *Gideon v. Wainwright* and granted Clarence Gideon a new trial. That same month, 23-year-old Ernesto Miranda was arrested in Phoenix, Arizona.

A Troubled Childhood

Miranda's childhood had not been an easy one. Ernesto Arturo Miranda was born to Mexican immigrants in Mesa, Arizona, on March 9, 1941. When he was five, his mother died, and his father soon remarried. Ernesto did not get along with his father, his stepmother, or his brothers. He often got in trouble at school, the Queen of Peace Grammar

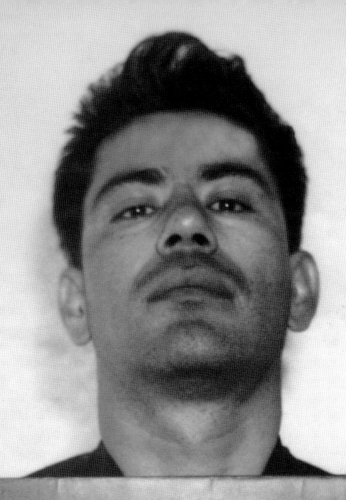

ARIZONA STATE PRISON
FLORENCE, ARIZONA

2 7 5 5 5 4-10-'67

By age 23, Miranda had been involved in a number
of criminal activities.

School in Mesa, and seldom went to class. The eighth grade was his last complete year of education.

Miranda committed his first **felony**, car theft, at the age of 13. Over the next five years, he was arrested for burglary, attempted rape, assault, voyeurism (Peeping Tom activities), and suspicion of armed robbery. At the age of 18, Miranda joined the US Army. However, his behavior did not change. He served time in hard labor for charges of voyeurism and being absent without leave before being dishonorably discharged. Then, he was arrested for auto theft and did time in federal prison. After being released from a prison in Lompoc, California, he met Twila Hoffman and moved in with her and her two children. A year later, the couple had a daughter of their own and moved to Mesa to find jobs. In August 1962, Miranda got a job with United Produce in Phoenix. This was the most stable position he had ever held. But when he was not at work, he roamed the streets of Phoenix sometimes looking for women who were alone and vulnerable.

felony—A serious crime, which usually carries a minimum sentence of one or more years in prison.

DISHONORABLE DISCHARGE

When someone in the US military commits a crime or has extremely bad behavior, the military may try that person at a general court-martial made up of a military judge and at least five members of the military. If convicted, the sentence can include a dishonorable discharge. The person must leave the military and forfeit all veterans' benefits. In some states, those who have been dishonorably discharged from the military may be denied their civil rights.

Abduction

Just before midnight on Saturday, March 2, 1963, 18-year-old Jane Smith (not her real name) left the Paramount Theater in downtown Phoenix. Her job at the concession stand was over for the night, so she boarded a city bus to head home. Smith got off at the corner of Seventh Street and Marlette, near her house on Citrus Way. In this neighborhood, rows of small adobe houses lined the streets, and poverty and crime were common. She noticed a car parked in a lot behind a ballet school on Marlette. As she walked, the car drove by and nearly hit her. The driver, Miranda, then parked the car, got out, walked up to her on the sidewalk, and grabbed her. He told Smith not to scream; he was not going to hurt her. Miranda held her hands behind her back, covered her mouth, and pushed her toward his car. Shoving her into the backseat, face down, he bound Smith's hands behind her back and tied her ankles together. Pressing a sharp object against her neck, he said, "Feel this."[1]

For the next 20 minutes, Miranda drove the car out of the city and into the Arizona desert while Smith lay crying on the backseat. Miranda repeatedly said, "Keep quiet, and I won't hurt you."[2] In the desert, with no one around, Miranda stopped the car, untied his captive, and told her to take off her clothes. When she refused, he did it for her. Then he raped her. Smith later testified,

> *I was pushing against him with my hands. I kept screaming. I was trying to get away but he was a lot stronger than I was, and I couldn't do anything.*[3]

RAPE IN PHOENIX

Reports of rape were common in Phoenix during the 1960s. In 1963, the year Miranda was accused of raping Smith, 152 rapes were reported in the city. This was 20 percent more than the previous year and 33 percent more than 1961. In 1970, 300 rapes were reported, nearly twice as many as the year Smith was assaulted.[4]

When Miranda was finished, he ordered Smith to give him all her money, but she only had four dollars in her purse. He took it all.

While Smith dressed in the backseat, Miranda drove back to the city, close to the spot where he had abducted her. He let Smith out of the car and drove away. Smith claimed that as he drove away, Miranda called out to her, "Please pray for me."[5] Crying, Smith ran home and reached her front door appearing as though she had been in a fight. Smith told her family what had happened, and they called police. Police officers arrived at her house at 2:08 a.m. After questioning her briefly, police officers took the extremely distraught young woman to Good Samaritan Hospital for medical care.

The Lineup

At the hospital, Smith told police everything she could remember about her abductor. She described him as Hispanic, approximately 27 or 28 years old, five feet eleven inches (1.8 m) tall, and approximately 175 pounds (79.4 kg). She remembered him as slender with medium skin color and short, black hair. He wore a white T-shirt, jeans, and dark-rimmed glasses. After Smith had been released from the hospital, police put together a lineup of men who came close to her description, but she could not positively identify any of them. She also could not tell the police much about her abductor's car other than that it was an older, four-door sedan. She remembered it smelling like paint or turpentine inside and that there was a circular rope attached to the back of the front seat. Smith thought this rope was something for passengers to grab on to when getting out of the car.

Two Similar Crimes

On Monday, March 4, Sergeant Seymour Nealis, head of the Crimes Against Persons Detail for the Phoenix Police

Department, assigned Smith's case to Detective Carroll Cooley, an organized, experienced investigator. Nealis and Cooley connected the crime to two other similar assaults against women in the past four months. All three women had similar descriptions of their assailant, including the way he acted and spoke. They all described a similar weapon, most likely a small knife.

Later, as police continued questioning Smith, she became unsure of the man's nationality and changed the details of her abduction. The police became skeptical and doubted she had even been raped. One of her brothers-in-law later explained to police that Smith might have been confused because she was "a little slow."[6] Smith had the IQ of a 12- or 13-year-old and had not completed high school.

Suspicious Sedan

Approximately a week after Smith's rape, the search for a suspect reached a dead end. Police were about to close the case, but then there was a breakthrough. Smith was still working at the Paramount Theater, taking a bus, and walking three blocks home. But now, her brother-in-law met her every night at the bus stop to ensure she made it home safely. One night, her brother-in-law spotted an older Packard sedan driving slowly around the area. He made note of the Arizona license plate number. When Smith got off the bus, the two of them began walking and saw the car, which had stopped alongside the road. As they approached it, the driver quickly drove off. Police traced the license plate to an Oldsmobile that had not been in the Phoenix area on March 2 or 3. As they checked similar license plate numbers, DFL-317 came up as a 1953 green Packard registered to 29-year-old Twila Hoffman, who lived nearby in Mesa. When Cooley contacted Hoffman, she admitted she was living with a man who often borrowed her car. His name was Ernesto Miranda.

On the morning of March 13, 1963, police officers Cooley and Wilfred Young arrived at the house where Hoffman and Miranda lived. A 1953 green Packard with a loop of a rope attached to the back of the front seat was parked in the driveway. Hoffman answered the door and woke up Miranda, who had been asleep after working a 12-hour shift. He agreed to go with the officers to the police station for questioning. "I didn't know whether I had a choice," he said later.[7]

Miranda was immediately put in a lineup with three other men, all Hispanics and of similar height

Twila Hoffman's car, where Miranda's crime took place

Smith was not certain the man who attacked her was in the police lineup. Miranda is on the far left.

and appearance. Smith viewed the four men through a one-way glass. She said the man on the far left—Miranda—looked similar to her abductor, but she was not sure. The police would use this statement to mislead Miranda.

The Interrogation Room

Interrogation Room Number 2 at the Phoenix Police Department was soundproofed and isolated. It contained three chairs for Cooley, Young, and Miranda. "How did I do?"[8] Miranda asked about the lineup. Cooley lied, saying, "You flunked."[9] Before long, Miranda confessed to raping Jane Smith. He also admitted to trying to rape another woman and robbing a third woman between November 1962 and March 1963.

> " Once they get you in a little room and they start badgering you one way or the other, "you better tell us . . . or we're going to throw the book at you" . . . And I haven't had any sleep since the day before. I'm tired. I just got off work, and they have me and they are interrogating me. They mention first one crime, then another one, they are certain I am the person . . . knowing what a penitentiary is like, a person has to be frightened, scared."[11]
>
> —*ERNESTO MIRANDA*

Cooley and Young then brought Smith to the doorway of the interrogation room. One of the officers asked Miranda if this was the girl he had raped.

VOLUNTARY CONFESSIONS

Today, a voluntary confession is defined as an admission of guilt that a suspect makes and is not given under circumstances that make the confession unreliable. The confession cannot be obtained by unacceptable interrogation methods. For example, the admission cannot be a result of coercion, force, threats, promises, or intimidation. If a confession is not voluntary, it cannot be admitted into court as evidence. However, a defendant may still be convicted if there is sufficient additional evidence to prove guilt beyond a reasonable doubt.

He replied, "That's the girl."[10] Cooley asked Miranda if he would put his story in writing, and he agreed. At the top of the paper, a typed statement declared that Miranda confessed voluntarily, understood his rights, and knew what he said could be used against him. Miranda wrote a full confession, but he was never told he did not have to make statements that would incriminate himself, according to the Fifth Amendment of the US Constitution. He was never told he could have a lawyer. The officers later claimed Miranda should have known his rights since he had already served prison time. They testified Miranda's confessions were completely voluntary and not coerced in any way.

Miranda's arrest, interrogation, and confession launched a heated debate that would last for decades. The events of March 13, 1963, in the Phoenix Police Department's Interrogation Room Number 2 became the catalyst for drastic changes that eventually affected law enforcement, criminal arrest procedures, and criminal trials across the United States. ∼

Chapter 4

Trial and First Appeal

In 1963, Maricopa County appointed 73-year-old attorney Alvin Moore to represent Miranda at his trial for burglary, kidnapping, and rape. The county paid Moore $100 for his services. Moore was not fond of criminal trials and avoided them as he got older. He claimed that when "in close association with criminals, you begin to think like criminals."[1] But recently, as a matter of civic duty, he had signed up to be a public defender. Moore had a good record in criminal court. He had represented 35 defendants on charges of rape, and only one had been convicted.

Insanity Plea

Miranda's trial was set for May 14, 1963, in the Maricopa Superior Court before Judge Yale McFate. The day before trial, Moore filed a notice with the court that he would attempt to prove Miranda was **legally insane** at the time of the crime. Judge McFate immediately postponed the trial and appointed two psychiatrists to examine Miranda. The psychiatrists examined Miranda and gave their report to the court: although the defendant was mentally abnormal, he understood the charges against him, understood what would happen if he was found guilty, and was able to assist his lawyer in his own defense. Moore's findings did not meet the

legally insane—Having a defect of reasoning that prevents a defendant from knowing his or her crime was wrong.

definition of legal insanity, and the trial was rescheduled for June 19.

The Trial

State of Arizona v. Ernesto Miranda was a simple trial with only four witnesses: Officer Cooley, Officer Young, Jane Smith, and her sister, who had seen Smith the night of the rape. On the witness stand, Smith spoke very softly and broke down emotionally several times. Each time, the trial was stopped while she gained her composure. Moore called no witnesses to the stand on behalf of the defendant. Miranda did not testify, and the only item entered into evidence was Miranda's handwritten, signed confession.

Moore claimed his client's confession was coerced; therefore, it should not be admitted as evidence. Moore also argued that Miranda's constitutional rights had been violated. He stated, "We object because the Supreme Court of the United States says a man is entitled to an attorney at the time of his arrest."[2] He argued the US Supreme Court had already ruled on this issue in *Gideon v. Wainwright*, but Judge McFate overruled Moore on the grounds that *Gideon* did not apply. He stated that *Gideon* gave defendants the right to an attorney at trial— not at the time of the arrest. The judge then allowed Miranda's confession to be entered into evidence.

In Moore's final statement to the jury, he presented his only argument: Smith did not have any bruises or injuries after the rape. At that time, Arizona law required rape victims to "resist to the utmost," and Moore stated that Smith had not done so.[3] Moore told the jury the evidence showing that Smith had resisted to the best of her ability was not strong enough. Due to the lack of such evidence, it would be wrong to send Miranda to prison.

When the final arguments were over, Judge McFate gave the jurors clear instructions. Although he allowed them to consider Miranda's confession, they should not use it as evidence if they believed his confession was involuntary or police had coerced him to confess through violence or threats. The judge added:

> *The fact that a defendant was under arrest at the time he made the confession, or that he was not at the time represented by counsel or that he was not told that any statement he might make could or would be used against him, in and of themselves, will not render such confessions involuntary.*[4]

McFate's directions to the jury denied them the opportunity to decide if Miranda's constitutional rights had been violated. It took the jury of nine men and three women five hours to find Miranda guilty of kidnapping and rape. On June 27, Miranda received a sentence of 20 to 30 years in prison for each charge. The sentences would be served concurrently, or at the same time. Miranda was immediately transported to the Arizona State Prison in Florence, Arizona.

The First Appeal

Miranda's attorney believed the interrogation methods of the Phoenix Police Department had violated Miranda's constitutional rights. He also believed the judge had made mistakes at the trial. Judge McFate had ordered the jury to consider Miranda's confession as long as they believed it was voluntary—a fact the jury would have had a difficult time determining without further help from the judge. Because of this, Moore strongly felt his client had not been given a fair trial. Several months later, Moore filed an appeal with the Arizona Supreme Court, the state's highest court at the time.

In the appeal, Moore claimed Miranda's confession was not voluntary and should not have been allowed

ARIZONA COURT SYSTEM

Until 1965, Arizona had only two courts: the superior court for trials and the supreme court for appeals. The court of appeals was established in 1965 to handle the first level of appeals after trial in superior court. The Arizona Supreme Court became responsible for the second level of appeals, if necessary, and became the court of last resort. Because Miranda filed his appeal in 1963, he had only one level of state appeal, the supreme court.

into evidence. He also stated that Miranda was denied assistance of counsel and was not warned what he said could be used against him. Moore wrote, "We are objecting because the Supreme Court of the United States says the man is entitled to an attorney at the time of his arrest."[6] Moore asked the court to reverse Miranda's conviction.

Escobedo v. Illinois

The Arizona Supreme Court took more than a year and a half to rule on Miranda's appeal, which was an unusually long time. In the meantime, the US Supreme Court was hearing another case—*Escobedo v. Illinois*. This case drew attention to the same issue of whether the accused has the right to an attorney while being questioned by police. While it was standard procedure in most states to offer an attorney to a defendant for trial, it was not standard practice during a police interrogation. Danny Escobedo had asked for an attorney while he was being questioned. His lawyer was present at the police station and asked to see Escobedo. Police denied both men's requests. The case was appealed to the US Supreme Court. On June 22, 1964, the Supreme Court handed down its decision. Justice Goldberg, who wrote on behalf of the 5–4 majority, stated that under certain circumstances, a custodial suspect, or a suspect in police custody, has the right to an attorney when being questioned by police. He went on to write:

> Under the circumstances of this case, where a police investigation is no longer a general inquiry into an unsolved crime but has begun to focus on a particular suspect in police custody who has been refused an opportunity to consult with his counsel and who has not been warned of his constitutional right to keep silent, the accused has been denied the assistance of counsel in violation of the Sixth and Fourteenth Amendments, and no statement extracted by the police during the interrogation may be used against him at a trial.[7]

The *Escobedo* decision was open to interpretation, and the Arizona Supreme Court did not believe the case applied to *Miranda*. Escobedo had requested a lawyer and been denied that opportunity; Miranda had not requested a lawyer at all. On April 22, 1965, the Arizona Supreme Court denied Miranda's appeal. The justices interpreted *Escobedo* as stating that, in order for a custodial suspect to be denied his or her constitutional rights, the suspect must specifically request and then be refused an opportunity to consult a lawyer. Justice Ernest W. McFarland, who wrote the appellate court's 21-page opinion, stated Miranda "had not requested and been

ESCOBEDO AND HIS LAWYER

Shortly after Danny Escobedo was arrested on January 20, 1960, his lawyer showed up at police headquarters to see his client. He asked and was denied his request three times. He even approached the chief of police and asked to see his client. The chief said he could not see Escobedo because they had not finished questioning him. The attorney recalled, "[F]or a second or two, I spotted him [Escobedo] in an office in the Homicide Bureau. The door was open, and I could see through the office. . . . I waved to him and he waved back and then the door was closed, by one of the officers at Homicide."[8] Escobedo later testified he had "repeatedly asked to speak to his lawyer, and . . . the police said that his lawyer 'didn't want to see' him."[9]

denied assistance of counsel" and his confession was thus admissible.[10] McFarland also stated, "[a] Confession may be admissible when made without an attorney if it is voluntary and does not violate constitutional rights of defendant."[11]

The court concluded Miranda's confession was, indeed, voluntary. Since he had been arrested several times before, he was certainly familiar with "legal proceedings and his rights in court."[12] The appellate court stated the lower trial court did not make any errors and had correctly admitted Miranda's confession into evidence. The court upheld Miranda's convictions.

Throughout the United States, the *Escobedo* decision became increasingly unpopular. Courts were not sure how to interpret it. Some judges interpreted the ruling narrowly and believed the circumstances of any case had to be almost identical to Escobedo's arrest in order to apply. Other courts interpreted the decision broadly and often ruled in favor of defendants who should not have been acquitted. Many people feared the *Escobedo* decision would set dangerous criminals free on technicalities. Police complained that *Escobedo* would make it nearly impossible to get a confession. Prosecutors also worried about *Escobedo*. At the 1965

Danny Escobedo was freed from prison after the
Supreme Court overturned his conviction.

winter conference of the National Association of District Attorneys in Houston, Texas, one official predicted,

> Someday, I guess, the Court will rule that we can't talk to a suspect without first giving him a lawyer. . . . When that happens, believe me, the ball game is over. You're going to see a lot of killers and rapists walking out of police stations with thumb to nose.[13]

What exactly did the US Supreme Court mean by its *Escobedo* decision? How should the lower courts interpret it—narrowly or broadly? How would it affect every police department and investigator in the nation? It would take another US Supreme Court case—*Miranda v. Arizona*—to clarify those issues. ~

Chapter 5

Petitioning the US Supreme Court

osing his appeal in the Arizona Supreme Court meant Miranda had only one more way to appeal his case. He would have to file a petition for a writ of certiorari with the United States Supreme Court. His attorney, however, did not want to file the petition or represent Miranda any longer. Moore was tired and old and did not want to go through another appeal.

After two years in the maximum-security prison in Florence, Miranda decided to write his own petition without the help of a lawyer. In June 1965, he mailed a handwritten petition for a writ of certiorari to the clerk of the US Supreme Court in

Washington DC. This was an interesting time to file an appeal concerning constitutional or civil rights. In the 1960s, the US Supreme Court was known for its aggressive, bold decisions regarding individual rights and extreme social reforms.

The court used its powers as the **judicial branch** of the US government to achieve more social changes than any other Supreme Court in US history. The court's opinions were based on a broad, liberal interpretation of the Constitution, especially the Bill of Rights. As often is the case, the nature of the court reflected the character and beliefs of its presiding judge, Chief Justice Earl Warren.

The Warren Court

As a young man, Earl Warren had worked for the Southern Pacific Railroad and saw firsthand how the large, powerful railroad company did not afford workers their rights. After graduating from law school in 1914, Warren worked as a California prosecutor, bringing

judicial branch—One of three branches of the federal government; it includes the nation's court system and decides if laws are constitutional.

Earl Warren was chief justice of the Supreme Court from 1953 to 1969.

criminals to trial and gathering sufficient evidence to convict them. He believed in fairness and worked to establish a public defender's office in California for people who could not afford an attorney. His passion for constitutional rights for all individuals shaped his life. It also affected how he later ruled on cases brought before him during his 16 years as chief justice of the Supreme Court. Warren was 62 years old and the popular governor of California when President Dwight D. Eisenhower appointed him to the Supreme Court in 1953.

During Warren's first Supreme Court term, the court took on *Brown v. Board of Education*, which brought an end to segregation of schools in 1954. In 1961, the court began a string of years that are commonly referred to as the "heyday of the Warren Court."[1] From 1961 through 1967, the court ruled on hundreds of cases challenging issues such as civil rights, racial desegregation, separation of church and state, freedom of speech, and police arrest procedures.

The Warren court required defendants to be protected by their constitutional rights, no matter the state in which they were being tried. Throughout the history of the United States, American citizens were held to two legal standards: federal law and state law. If citizens violated federal laws, such as kidnapping, treason, and narcotics violations, they were tried in federal courts and were fully protected by the Bill of Rights. However, citizens who broke state laws were tried in state courts and were not protected by the first ten amendments unless the state had instituted its own similar list of rights or the US Supreme Court had ruled a particular amendment was fundamental under the Fourteenth Amendment.

Most of the decisions of the Warren court were based on the Fourteenth Amendment. The amendment was originally adopted to force Southern states to comply with the Constitution and give equal rights to former slaves. But as time went by, it became the basis for expanding constitutional rights to the responsibility of the states. Section 1 of the Fourteenth Amendment states:

> *No State shall make or enforce any law which shall abridge the privileges or immunities of citizens of the United States; nor shall any State deprive any person of life, liberty, or property, without due process of law; nor deny to any person within its jurisdiction the equal protection of the laws.*[2]

THE WARREN COURT

In Earl Warren's 16 years as chief justice, from 1953 to 1969, the Supreme Court ruled on 1,750 cases. According to Warren, his most important decisions were the following:

- *Brown v. Board of Education* (1954)—banned racial segregation in public schools.
- *Baker v. Carr* (1962)—protected the rights of voters and the way voting districts are divided.
- *Gideon v. Wainwright* (1963)—gave the accused the right to free counsel if he or she cannot afford a lawyer.

In state courts, where burglary, rape, murder, and such are tried, defendants were not always protected by their basic constitutional rights. The Warren court, however, declared it was the responsibility of the states to follow the first ten amendments, especially the right to freedom of speech, the protection against self-incrimination, and the right to assistance of counsel. During the heyday of the Warren court, the justices ruled time after time that the Fourteenth Amendment obligated the states to ensure constitutional rights. State courts had to guarantee every citizen due process of law, which included the rights of the accused under the Fifth and Sixth amendments. In this environment, Miranda filed the case that became *Miranda v. Arizona* with the Supreme Court of the United States.

Robert Corcoran and the ACLU

After Miranda's petition to the Supreme Court, someone was ready to snatch up the case, file it again, and ensure it made it to the nation's highest court. In 1965, Robert J. Corcoran was in charge of the Phoenix office of the ACLU. When Corcoran learned of the Arizona appellate court's decision on *Miranda*, he believed it was just the case to strengthen and clarify the ever-controversial *Escobedo* decision.

After Moore declined taking the case to the US Supreme Court, Corcoran called several lawyers before he found one who would file the *Miranda* appeal. John Flynn was a leading criminal defense lawyer at one of Phoenix's largest law firms. He was well known in Phoenix for his extraordinary final arguments. It was said that the courtroom was always packed for Flynn's final address to the jury.

Needing help with the *Miranda* case, Flynn asked attorney John Frank to join him. Frank was an appellate lawyer in the same firm and an expert on constitutional law. Frank would write the **brief**, and Flynn would speak

Well-known attorney John Flynn agreed to help represent Miranda in his appeal to the Supreme Court.

before the Supreme Court justices. Neither lawyer would receive any money for appealing the case; their law firm would pay all the expenses. When Corcoran wrote to Miranda telling him he had found two lawyers to appeal his case pro bono, at no cost, Miranda responded enthusiastically in a letter:

brief—A document that establishes the legal arguments of a case.

Your letter . . . has made me very happy. To know that someone has taken an interest in my case, has increased my moral [sic] enormously. . . . I would appreciate if you or either Mr. Flynn keep me informed of any and all results. I also want to thank you and Mr. Flynn for all that you are doing for me.³

Flynn and Frank

Flynn was passionate about the law. He did not care whether Miranda was guilty or innocent. He later stated:

I fought [the Miranda case] on technicalities of the law, constitutional grounds, protected every right he possibly had. . . . That's what he's entitled to. And that's exactly what a person who's accused is entitled to, whether he's guilty or whether he's innocent. . . . That's what our whole system is structured around.⁴

Frank did not try to establish Miranda's guilt or innocence. Rather, he focused on the Constitution, on an individual's constitutional rights, and on the issues and controversies the Supreme Court should resolve.

Flynn and Frank agreed on their purpose—they were fighting for the constitutional rights of the accused.

PRO BONO PUBLICO

The term *pro bono publico* (usually just pro bono) means "for the public good." Lawyers typically do a certain amount of work for free and consider it a public service. The ethical rules of the American Bar Association state:

> *Every lawyer has a professional responsibility to provide legal services to those unable to pay. A lawyer should aspire to render at least (50) hours of pro bono publico legal services per year.*[5]

However, they disagreed on which aspects of the Bill of Rights they should focus on. They narrowed it down to the Fifth and Sixth amendments. The appeal would focus either on self-incrimination or assistance of counsel. They finally agreed on the Sixth Amendment, which guarantees that the accused may have the assistance of counsel. Flynn and Frank would raise a specific question—*when* should a suspect be advised of his or her right to consult an attorney?

In early summer 1965, Flynn and Frank composed a brief to accompany the petition sent to the Supreme Court. The brief was only nine pages long and just 2,500 words, but it was packed with details and logic. It explained how Miranda, now called the petitioner, had been denied his rights under the Fifth, Sixth, and Fourteenth amendments. The brief stated,

> The cause of due process is ill-served when a disturbed, little-educated [impoverished man] is sentenced to lengthy prison terms largely on the basis of a confession which he gave without being first advised of his right to counsel.[6]

The brief also asked the court to decide whether police could assume the accused knew about his or her right to counsel or whether the police were obligated to advise the suspect of that basic right.

THE WRONG AMENDMENT

As it turned out, Miranda's attorneys had made a mistake. They chose the wrong amendment. In spite of the court's previous focus on the Sixth Amendment with *Escobedo*, the court would base its *Miranda* decision on the Fifth Amendment and the right against self-incrimination. The very first paragraph of the court's opinion stated:

> *We deal with the admissibility of statements obtained from an individual who is subjected to custodial police interrogation and the necessity for procedures which assure that the individual is accorded his privilege under the Fifth Amendment to the Constitution not to be compelled to incriminate himself.[7]*

The attorneys also asked the court to end the legal confusion caused by *Escobedo*. They wanted resolution "so that the current widely conflicting treatment of a basic constitutional right can be resolved and substantial and similar justice attained by all accused persons wherever they live."[8] Flynn and Frank attached several items to the brief. These included Miranda's petition **in forma pauperis** along with an **affidavit** confirming his poverty and copies of the transcripts from the Arizona trial and appeal. The clerk of the US Supreme Court received the package on July 16, 1965.

A Flood of Petitions

By October, the US Supreme Court was flooded with more than 100 petitions addressing the issues in *Escobedo*. These had been filed over the prior 18 months by defendants from all over the country and some federal courts. It was the job of the law clerks to identify similar cases, group them together, and then set them aside for the justices to review later.

affidavit—A statement made under oath, witnessed by an individual with legal authority.

in forma pauperis—As a poor person; having legal fees waived due to insufficient funds.

THE SUPREME COURT BUILDING

The US Supreme Court did not have its own building until 1935. For 146 years, the court met in a variety of places, including space in the Merchants Exchange Building in New York City, the State House in Philadelphia, Pennsylvania, and the US Capitol in Washington DC. In 1929, Chief Justice William Howard Taft convinced Congress to approve a permanent building for the court. The imposing building, located near the US Capitol, was built between 1932 and 1935. Carved above the entrance are the words Equal Justice Under Law.[9]

On November 22, 1965, the nine justices of the Supreme Court met in a private room to discuss all the petitions—approximately 1,600—filed over the past year. The justices considered each one; it did not matter if the return address on the envelope was a prestigious law firm or a prison. But a petition had to involve a significant federal matter, a constitutional issue, in order for the Supreme Court justices to hear the case.

Petitions involving *Escobedo*, were grouped together. The justices intended to choose one petition to clear up the confusion over *Escobedo* and, at the same time, solve the issues in the remaining cases. But to everyone's surprise, the justices did not choose just one petition; they chose four to rule on collectively. Whatever decision

ESCOBEDO ON *TIME*

The cover of the April 29, 1966, edition of *Time* magazine pictured Danny Escobedo's front and side police mug shots with his name underneath. A blue diagonal strip across the upper right-hand corner contained the only words: "Moving the Constitution Into the Police Station."[10]

the court made would apply to all. The four cases were *Miranda v. Arizona, Vignera v. New York, Westover v. United States,* and *California v. Stewart.* The court would hear the legal arguments for *Miranda* first, and thus, the name of the four combined cases became *Miranda v. Arizona.* Little did anyone know how significant this case would become. ～

Chapter 6

Landmark Decision

Flynn and Frank had made it over their first big hurdle in *Miranda v. Arizona*—the highest court had agreed to review it. Now it was time to file another legal brief, a longer document summarizing all the facts of the case and the legal basis for their argument. They filed the brief with the US Supreme Court on January 19, 1966.

The document described in detail what had occurred in the Phoenix Police Department's Interrogation Room Number 2 on March 13, 1963. It also discussed similar cases, from *Powell* to *Escobedo*, and how they applied to *Miranda*. Finally,

The Supreme Court Building, located in Washington DC, houses the highest court in the nation.

the brief explained how the case related to the Sixth Amendment:

> *The day is here to recognize the full meaning of the Sixth Amendment. . . . "[A suspect] requires the guiding hand of counsel at every step in the proceedings against him." When Miranda stepped into Interrogation Room 2, he had only the guiding hand of Officers Cooley and Young.*[1]

Providing an attorney after the arrest was too late, the brief claimed. The accused needs legal advice when it matters—after the suspect is arrested and before police begin an interrogation.

More Legal Briefs

Two weeks later, Gary Nelson, assistant attorney general for the state of Arizona, filed a brief on behalf of the respondent, the state of Arizona. He argued *Miranda* should not be compared to *Escobedo* and claimed Miranda's circumstances were extremely different. Miranda had not requested a lawyer; Escobedo had. Miranda had been arrested many times before; it was the first offense for Escobedo. Miranda had been informed of his rights under the Constitution; Escobedo had not. Nelson wrote, "[The cases are] not equal and there is no Constitutional reason for this Court to equate them."[2] He asked the court not to expand the meaning of *Escobedo* too much or "a serious problem in the enforcement of our criminal law will occur."[3]

Lawyers in the three companion cases also filed briefs on behalf of the other petitioners. Other briefs were sent to the court by individuals or organizations interested in influencing the outcome of the case. Called amici curiae, Latin for "friend of the court," the briefs were filed by interested parties offering opinions

> " So long as we have enough people in this country willing to fight for their rights, we'll be called a democracy."[5]
> —*ACLU FOUNDER ROGER BALDWIN*

or advice. The ACLU, the National District Attorneys Association, and the National Association of State Attorneys General all filed briefs. The state of New York filed an amicus curiae brief, asking the court to "go slow," not to interfere with the states, and to let states establish their own laws for protecting suspects.[4] The briefs included a wide variety of viewpoints and ideas about an individual's constitutional rights.

In the Court Chamber

On Monday, February 28, 1966, approximately six weeks after Miranda's brief was first filed, Flynn was in Washington DC. Early that morning, he walked past the 16 marble columns at the entrance to the US Supreme Court Building and strode through the two enormous 17-short ton (15-metric ton) bronze sliding doors. He walked down the hall and entered the court chamber where oral arguments would be heard that day.

As the nine Supreme Court justices entered the room, wearing long, black robes, the marshal made the customary announcement,

> *Oyez! Oyez! Oyez! All persons having business before the honorable, the Supreme Court of the United States, are admonished to draw near and give their attention, for the court is now sitting. God save the United States and this honorable court.*[6]

The court chamber was packed that day because the *Miranda* case was scheduled immediately after *Sheppard v. Maxwell*, a widely publicized case involving Doctor Samuel Sheppard, a man convicted of murdering his wife.

OPEN SEATING

Oral arguments in the US Supreme Court are open to the public. Seating is on a first-come, first-seated basis. Before a session begins, two lines form outside the courthouse. One is for people who want to attend an entire oral argument; the other is the three-minute line for those who wish to briefly observe the court in session.

Early in the afternoon, Flynn spoke to the justices of the Supreme Court. He was allotted 30 minutes to present his case to the nine men who sat elevated high above him. It was Flynn's only chance to argue his case on behalf of Miranda and, in essence, on behalf of all US citizens. He began in the traditional way: "Mr. Chief Justice, may it please the Court."[7] Then he went on to recap the details of the case—Miranda's crimes, his arrest, the lineup, and the interrogation.

Flynn described how Miranda denied his guilt at the beginning of the interrogation and then admitted to the crimes two hours later. The confession, he emphasized, took place in an isolated room with two investigators and Miranda. No attorney was in the room, and Miranda was not allowed to leave.

THE COURT AND COERCED CONFESSIONS

As early as the 1930s, the US Supreme Court ruled on whether coerced confessions violated a person's Fourteenth Amendment rights to due process of law. In 1936, the court ruled in *Brown v. Mississippi* that a confession obtained by beating or whipping a defendant might be false. Introducing such a confession into evidence could result in the conviction of an innocent person. In *Ashcraft v. Tennessee* in 1944, the defendant was not beaten but was questioned nonstop for 36 hours. The court reversed his conviction since his confession was acquired in an unacceptable manner. In the 1950s, the court began ruling that confessions elicited through psychological methods that "overbear the will" of the defendant were not admissible in court.[9]

Flynn told the justices,

> *I believe the record indicates that at no time during the interrogation and prior to his oral confession was [Miranda] advised either of his rights to remain silent, his right to counsel, or of his right to consult with counsel. . . . The defendant was then asked to sign a confession, to which he agreed.*[8]

Flynn further argued that if a confession was made during the interrogation, then "the mere formality of supplying counsel to Ernest Miranda at the time of trial . . . would really be nothing more than a mockery of his Sixth Amendment right."[10] By that time, Flynn inferred, it was too late to receive important advice from an attorney.

Throughout Flynn's oral argument, justices interrupted him with pointed questions. Justice Potter Stewart was the first to challenge Flynn on the right to counsel and asked exactly *when* a suspect had that right. Justice Hugo Black followed with a question to Flynn about the Fifth Amendment:

> *You have said several times . . . that in determining whether or not a person shall be compelled to be a witness against himself, that it might depend to some extent on his literacy or his illiteracy, his wealth or his lack of wealth, his standing or his lack of standing—why does that have anything to do with it? Why does the Amendment not protect the rich, as well as the poor; the literate, as well as the illiterate?*[11]

Flynn responded that the amendment does, in fact, protect everyone if a suspect has the knowledge and mental capacity to understand his or her rights. He added, "if [the accused] is too ignorant to know that he has the Fifth Amendment right, then certainly literacy has something to do with it, Your Honor."[12]

DIVERSITY IN THE SUPREME COURT

In the 1800s, every Supreme Court justice was a white male. In the mid-1900s, the court became more diverse. President Lyndon B. Johnson appointed the first African-American justice, Thurgood Marshall, in 1967. In 1981, President Ronald Reagan fulfilled his campaign promise to appoint a woman to the US Supreme Court by selecting Sandra Day O'Connor as the first female justice. President Barack Obama appointed the first Hispanic justice, Sonia Sotomayor, to the court in 2009.

The questions gave Flynn the perfect opportunity to make his case—many American citizens do not know about their Fifth Amendment rights. Someone has to tell them.

Nelson, the next person to address the justices, summed up his opposing argument by stating,

> I think if the extreme position is adopted that says [the accused] has to either have counsel at this stage or intelligently waive counsel, that a serious problem in the enforcement of our criminal law will occur. . . . When counsel is introduced at an interrogation, interrogation ceases immediately.[13]

Oral arguments continued into the next day. Duane Nedrud, representative for the National District

Attorney's Association, was the last person to address the court. He argued,

> *If this is to be our objective—to limit the use of the confession in criminal cases—then you are taking from the police the most important piece of evidence in every case that they bring before a court of justice. . . . Is this what we are looking for, to acquit Miranda because he did not have counsel?*[14]

Attorney Nelson had already stated almost the same thing earlier. Interrogation would stop, he claimed, except for what an attorney decides is best for the suspect. "Otherwise, counsel will not be doing his job."[15]

But the questions remained: When should the accused be allowed to have a lawyer? Should the rights of the Fifth Amendment apply outside the courtroom? Should an attorney be allowed in the interrogation room? Do the police have to inform the accused of the constitutional right to assistance of counsel? It would be up to the nine Supreme Court justices to answer those questions.

5–4 Split Decision

Three and a half months passed before the Supreme Court justices delivered their opinion on *Miranda*.

Chief Justice Earl Warren, *front center*, and the other eight justices who heard *Miranda v. Arizona* in 1965

It was a split 5–4 vote; five justices decided Miranda had been denied his constitutional rights. They voted to reverse the decisions of the Arizona courts and reverse his kidnapping and rape convictions. The opinion stated:

We reverse. From the testimony of the officers and by the admission of respondent, it is clear that Miranda was not in any way apprised of his right to consult with an attorney and to have one present during the interrogation, nor was his right not to be compelled to incriminate himself effectively protected in any other manner. Without these warnings, the statements were inadmissible.[16]

Four justices dissented: John M. Harlan II, Potter Stewart, Byron White, and Tom Clark. They were concerned that suspects would always demand a lawyer, and police officers would never be able to get a confession. They believed the other justices were going too far in their attempt to eliminate coercion.

Chief Justice Earl Warren wrote the majority opinion on behalf of the five justices who voted to reverse *Miranda*; it was common for the chief justice to write opinions in the most controversial cases. The other justices in the majority were Hugo Black, William O. Douglas, William J. Brennan Jr., and Abe Fortas.

On Monday, June 13, 1966, a large crowd gathered in the courtroom to hear Chief Justice Warren read the majority opinion aloud. He read for nearly an hour and did not omit any part of the 60-page document. The

THE RIGHT TO COUNSEL

The *Miranda* opinion clearly concluded that when Miranda was questioned, "statements were obtained from the defendant under circumstances that did not meet constitutional standards for protection of the privilege."[17] Unmistakably, the court decided Miranda had been denied his constitutional rights in Interrogation Room Number 2. Warren added, "Today, then, there can be no doubt that the Fifth Amendment privilege is available outside of criminal court proceedings, and serves to protect persons in all settings."[18] He thus gave any suspect taken into custody the right to be informed of his or her right to have an attorney present before or during an interrogation. If a suspect waived this right—as many did—the interrogation could continue. The opinion also set forth exactly what police officers were required to do.

dissenting justices followed by reading their opinions. In the Arizona State Prison in Florence, inmate number 27555—Miranda—was watching the news on television when he learned the Supreme Court had reversed his conviction.

A week later, the court ruled on a similar case, *Johnson v. New Jersey*. The question came up as to whether *Miranda* would apply retroactively to *Johnson*. Would hundreds of other prisoners be given new trials because they had confessed to their crimes without being warned of their constitutional rights? The Supreme Court said no. *Miranda* would not apply to any cases before the Supreme Court decision, dated June 13, 1966. However, police interrogation techniques would be changed forever. ~

Chapter 7
After the Ruling

The *Miranda* decision protected a person's Fifth Amendment rights more than ever before. The opinion stated: "when an individual is taken into custody or otherwise deprived of his freedom by the authorities in any significant way and is subjected to questioning, the privilege against self-incrimination is jeopardized."[1] The opinion also relied on the Sixth Amendment, the right to the assistance of counsel. But the justices focused on the Fifth Amendment. After all, they concluded, if someone is denied the assistance of an attorney, he or she is more likely to make self-incriminating statements.

The Supreme Court's opinion was very clear about statements made by a suspect in police custody:

> *The prosecution may not use statements . . . stemming from custodial interrogation of the defendant unless it demonstrates the use of procedural safeguards effective to secure the privilege against self-incrimination.*[2]

The opinion defined "custodial interrogation" as "questioning initiated by law enforcement officers after a person has been taken into custody or otherwise deprived of his freedom of action in any significant way."[3] The opinion then listed the "procedural safeguards," which are the specific processes that police officers have to follow to protect a suspect's Fifth Amendment rights.[4] Officers had to ensure a person taken into custody was informed of four specific constitutional rights. While an explicit reading of the rights was not necessarily required, stating these rights became part of every police officer's routine. These rights came to be called the Miranda warning or Miranda rights.

WHAT ABOUT THE OTHER PETITIONERS?

None of the three other petitioners in the *Miranda* companion cases automatically walked out of prison when the *Miranda* opinion was read. However, each petitioner in the three cases, *Vignera v. New York*, *Westover v. United States*, and *California v. Stewart*, had some sort of a second chance.

Michael Vignera pleaded guilty to a lesser charge of robbery and was sentenced to seven and a half to ten years in prison. However, he never went to prison because he was credited for time already served.

Carl Calvin Westover experienced two more trials, an appeal, and a third trial in California before his attorney convinced him to make a plea bargain for a reduced penalty. Westover pleaded guilty, and his sentence was reduced to ten years.

Roy Allen Stewart was granted a new trial in Los Angeles, California. Three years later, in July 1969, he was again convicted of first-degree murder and robbery even though his confession was not allowed into evidence. His original sentence, the death penalty, was changed to life in prison.

Miranda Warning

The justices repeatedly discussed law-enforcement procedures throughout the opinion. Near the end of the opinion, the justices summarized what police had to do:

Prior to any questioning, the person must be warned that:

He has the right to remain silent.

Anything he says can be used against him in a court of law.

He has the right to the presence of an attorney.

If he cannot afford an attorney one will be appointed for him prior to any questioning if he so desires.

After such warnings have been given, . . . the individual may knowingly and intelligently waive these rights and agree to answer questions or make a statement.[5]

Police departments and prosecutors across the nation were troubled by the *Miranda* decision. In Arizona, Maricopa County Attorney Robert Corbin called the decision a "black day for law enforcement."[6] Police had no choice but to incorporate the Miranda warning. They dutifully read or spoke a suspect's rights almost word for word from the court's opinion. Miranda warning cards were printed and distributed so police officers could carry them in their pockets and read them correctly to people they arrested—sometimes at the scene of the crime. Law enforcement and prosecutors did not want to leave anything out; if they did, a case could be reversed on appeal for just one violation of a suspect's Miranda rights. Typically, the police asked two questions at the end of the warning: "Do you understand each of these rights I have explained to you? Having these rights in mind, do you wish to talk to us now?"[7]

The *Miranda* opinion also allowed suspects to waive their Miranda rights, "provided the waiver is made voluntarily, knowingly, and intelligently."[8] When a person waived Miranda rights, the prosecutor faced the "heavy burden" of proving at trial that "the defendant

THOSE WHO NEED AN ATTORNEY MOST

In its *Miranda* opinion, the US Supreme Court relied on a California Supreme Court decision made one year before in 1965. In *People v. Dorado*, the California court ruled that the assistance of an attorney is a constitutional right; the accused does not have to formally request one. The court stated,

> The defendant who does not ask for counsel is the very defendant who most needs counsel. We cannot penalize a defendant who, not understanding his constitutional rights, does not make the formal request, and, by such failure, demonstrates his helplessness.[9]

knowingly and intelligently waived his privilege against self-incrimination and his right to retained or appointed counsel."[10] If a Miranda warning was not given, any evidence obtained during an interrogation could not be used against the defendant at trial.

A New Trial for Miranda

When the US Supreme Court delivered its opinion on June 13, 1966, Miranda expected to be released from prison immediately. He thought he was a free man. His father had bought a bottle of scotch to celebrate

DOUBLE JEOPARDY

The Fifth Amendment to the US Constitution protects a person from double jeopardy, or being tried twice for the same crime. It states that no person shall "be subject for the same offense to be twice put in jeopardy of life or limb."[11]

If a person is tried for a crime and found not guilty, he cannot be tried for that crime again, even if new evidence is found that would result in a conviction. However, when Miranda and the other petitioners received a second trial, it did not violate the Fifth Amendment. They were tried again for the same crimes because the Supreme Court ruled they had not received fair trials the first time and offered them another chance at a fair trial.

when his son walked out of prison and came home. But Miranda still had to serve out the rest of his sentence for burglary, which was not affected by the Supreme Court decision. He also had to return to the Superior Court of Maricopa County for a second trial on the charges of kidnapping and rape. This time, he would have to prove he had not been given the rights that now bore his own name—Miranda rights. As a result, his handwritten confession about what he did to Jane Smith could not be entered into evidence or used against him.

Miranda's second trial took place in February 1967. Smith was now married with a child. Once again, John Flynn represented Miranda, but there was a new prosecutor, Robert Corbin. A different judge, Lawrence K. Wren from Flagstaff, was brought to Phoenix specifically to hear the case. Convicting Miranda without his written confession was going to be very difficult for Corbin. However, he got a break when Twila Hoffman came to him with new information.

During the trial, Hoffman testified that three days after Miranda was arrested, he confessed to her that he had kidnapped and raped Smith. Hoffman also said Miranda had asked her to contact Smith and tell her that he would marry her—if Smith would drop the kidnapping and rape charges. Corbin now believed Hoffman's testimony would be enough to convict Miranda again.

A Second Verdict

Miranda's trial began on February 15, 1967, and lasted nine days. A jury of eight men and four women listened to testimony for only one day. On the other eight days, Flynn and Corbin argued with the judge over what evidence should be admissible. Flynn was especially concerned about Hoffman's testimony and pushed for getting the case dismissed on constitutional grounds. Judge Wren called it "a nine-day game of constitutional chess."[12]

In the end, Judge Wren allowed Hoffman's testimony. Hoffman told the jury she had visited Miranda in jail. While there, Miranda had admitted to her that he had kidnapped Smith, tied her up, then drove her out into the desert where he raped her. Hoffman also told the jury about Miranda's plan to bribe the victim with marriage so she would drop the charges. On March 1, the jury deliberated for over an hour before finding Miranda guilty of kidnapping and rape. Once again, he received a sentenced of 20 to 30 years in the Arizona State Prison at Florence. Later, Flynn told Judge Wren,

> *I goofed this case . . . I forgot about the jury. I forgot about the question of guilt or innocence and a proper presentation on that point because I became so wrapped up in getting it dismissed on constitutional questions.*[13]

For nearly six years, Miranda repeatedly applied for parole. The parole board granted his fourth request; he was released from prison in December 1972. For a while, Miranda made a small living selling autographed Miranda warning cards for one and a half dollars apiece. Before long, he was in trouble again with the law, which violated his parole. He was sentenced to one year in prison.

After being released from his latest prison stint, Miranda spent most of his time in an area of old

After the Supreme Court reversed Miranda's original conviction, Flynn represented Miranda in a second criminal trial in Phoenix.

downtown Phoenix known as the Deuce where he hung around bars and stayed in cheap hotels. On January 31, 1976, Miranda was stabbed to death in a bar fight. An accomplice to Miranda's murderer was apprehended, taken to the police station, and given his Miranda rights.

Although Miranda had lived most of his life without much notice, the *Miranda* case became one of the most well-known and most debated landmark decisions of the US Supreme Court. Its effects and its controversies would be felt for decades to come. ∼

Chapter 8

Reactions to *Miranda v. Arizona*

The *Miranda* opinion in June 1966 immediately caused public outrage and an uproar in police departments across the country. Law enforcement officials were not happy with the ruling and criticized the Supreme Court justices, claiming they were legislating from the bench. Police predicted a drop in conviction rates and an increase in crime.

Nonetheless, law enforcement agencies adapted to *Miranda*. It was a challenge for police officers across the United States to revise their arrest and interrogation procedures. Many officers resented the changes and mistrusted the Supreme Court. They believed their courage, intelligence, skills, and training were being questioned and that all rights now belonged to the suspect. One person noted that police officers viewed *Miranda* as a "slap at policemen everywhere . . . a personal rebuke."[1] Law enforcement officials felt as though their hands were tied and asked what they could do under *Miranda*.

Boston Police Commissioner Edmund L. McNamara stated, "criminal trials no longer will be a search for truth, but a search for technical error."[2] Chief of Police Richard Wagner of Cleveland, Ohio, was skeptical and wondered if police officers could ever get a statement from a suspect again. Los Angeles Police Chief William H. Parker believed *Miranda* would bring an end to the use of confessions to convict criminals.

CARROLL COOLEY, TEN YEARS LATER

Ten years after *Miranda*, Carroll Cooley, who interrogated Miranda, looked back on the Supreme Court decision. He was convinced *Miranda* had hindered police work. He believed *Miranda* allowed many guilty suspects to dodge the answers that would have convicted them.

On the other side of the debate, many said *Miranda* was necessary to protect an individual's constitutional rights. They claimed the ruling prevented police interrogations from bordering on physical or psychological torture. Supporters said the Miranda warning would cut down on the questionable practices police often used to draw out confessions.

> " I am so disgusted . . . with what we have to contend with in law enforcement since the US Supreme Court saw fit to so recklessly interpret the law to benefit lawbreakers, to misinterpret the will of our law makers, that I am resigning my position as chief of police."[3]
>
> —*A POLICE CHIEF IN RESPONSE TO THE MIRANDA DECISION*

Soft on Crime

Many judges and politicians criticized *Miranda*. Warren E. Burger, judge for the US Court of Appeals for the District of Columbia Circuit, openly condemned the Supreme Court for its rulings on *Miranda* and *Escobedo*. In the three years following *Miranda*, Burger essentially ignored the Supreme Court ruling in his own court. He upheld the convictions of 87 percent of the criminal cases that came before him on appeal. He regretted the cases he had to overturn due to confessions that were obviously inadmissible.

In 1967, Burger gave a controversial commencement address to the graduates of Ripon College in Wisconsin. His speech, titled crime and punishment, was an unusual topic for a graduation ceremony, but it became one of Burger's most important speeches. He stated that the criminal justice system, including the courts, had made it "very difficult to convict even those who are plainly guilty."[4] The media immediately circulated parts of his speech to newspapers and magazines. The issue quickly became a heated public discussion.

> There is no such thing as a voluntary statement. While the Supreme Court justices say it is, they have made it impossible to obtain one."[6]
>
> —*RICHARD WAGNER, CHIEF OF POLICE FOR CLEVELAND, OHIO*

In a 1968 speech to the Ohio Judicial Conference, Burger accused the Supreme Court of "revising the code of criminal procedure and evidence" instead of staying within its constitutional limits of judging cases on already existing laws.[5] In another speech, he questioned the Supreme Court's interpretation of the Fifth Amendment. "I am no longer sure . . . that the Fifth Amendment concept, in its present form and as presently applied and interpreted, has all the validity attributed to it."[7]

The Supreme Court justices had tried to avoid this kind of criticism when they wrote the *Miranda* opinion: "Our decision in no way creates a constitutional straitjacket which will handicap sound efforts at reform, nor is it intended to have this effect."[8] They also clearly stated the decision "is not intended to hamper the traditional function of police officers in investigating crime."[9] However, Burger and many others openly

NIXON DISAPPROVES

Burger's speeches attracted the attention of Richard M. Nixon, former vice president of the United States from 1953 to 1961 under President Dwight D. Eisenhower. Nixon was impressed with Burger's strong stance against crime and his open, candid disapproval of the Supreme Court. While campaigning for president of the United States in summer 1968, Nixon openly denounced the US Supreme Court for being "soft on crime."[10] He pointed to *Escobedo* and *Miranda* as decisions of an activist Court that "have had the effect of seriously hamstringing the peace forces in our society and strengthening the criminal forces."[11]

attacked the Supreme Court's rulings. Even Congress reacted to the Supreme Court, which many senators and representatives had come to disdain.

The Omnibus Crime Control Act of 1968

Criticism of the Supreme Court gained momentum in 1968. That year, an increasing number of ordinary citizens passionately opposed to *Miranda* claimed the Supreme Court was making laws instead of enforcing them. Congress had sensed the unpopularity of *Miranda*, and politicians were ready to take drastic measures. Democratic Senator John McClellan of Arkansas voiced his condemnation of *Miranda* to his fellow members of Congress:

> *This 5–4 decision is of such adverse significance to law enforcement that it demands early and thorough examination with a view to ascertaining just what legislation can and should be enacted to alleviate the obvious damage it will do to society.*[12]

Democratic Senator Samuel J. Ervin Jr. of North Carolina agreed with McClellan. He proclaimed,

> *Enough has been done for those who murder and rape and rob! . . . It is time to do something*

Senators prepare for hearings on the Omnibus Crime Control
and Safe Streets Act of 1968.

*for those who do not wish to be murdered or raped
or robbed.*[13]

Ervin brought attention to the recent drastic drop in the number of criminal confessions. He proposed a constitutional amendment that would allow voluntary confessions to be admitted into evidence in any court of law, regardless of whether suspects had been informed of or waived their right to an attorney. The Senate Judiciary Committee met to discuss the proposed amendment in the summer of 1966, but the amendment was never passed.

In the meantime, McClellan cosponsored a bill that would allow confessions to easily be admitted into evidence in federal courts. According to the proposed legislation, a voluntary confession was admissible as evidence in a federal court. The bill would nearly nullify *Miranda*, which was just what McClellan intended it to do. He also intended to stifle and limit the power of the US Supreme Court, which, he believed, had overstepped its constitutional boundaries as the judicial branch of government.

Senator McClellan's bill was brought before the Subcommittee on Criminal Laws and Procedures. McClellan invited numerous people to testify before the committee. Among them were police officers, prosecutors, state officials and legislators, and

US senators and representatives. Judge Wren, who had recently **presided** over Miranda's second trial, was also invited. Letters of support from citizens flooded McClellan's desk. Most were from police officers.

The outrage over *Miranda* was intense. Congress focused almost solely on *Miranda* and voluntary confessions while ignoring other issues such as ruthless tactics during police interrogations—commonly known as the third degree.

> Crime—the fact of crime and the fear of crime—marks the life of every American. We know its unrelenting pace: a forcible rape every 26 minutes, a robbery every five minutes, an aggravated assault every three minutes, a car theft every minute, a burglary every 28 seconds. We know its cost in dollars—some $27 billion annually."[14]
>
> —*PRESIDENT LYNDON B. JOHNSON, IN AN ADDRESS TO CONGRESS ON MARCH 9, 1966*

In January 1968, President Lyndon B. Johnson spoke out against rising crime in his State of the Union address to Congress: "There is no more urgent business before the Congress than to pass the [crime

presided—Heard and oversaw a trial.

bill] this year."[15] He also pushed for more funding to keep up the battle against crime. In May, the US Senate approved the crime bill, which became the Omnibus Crime Control and Safe Streets Act of 1968. The House of Representatives approved it in early June; President Johnson signed it into law on June 19, 1968.

The Omnibus Crime Act directed federal judges to admit into evidence any voluntary confessions or statements made by criminal defendants, regardless of whether they had received the Miranda warning. The legislation clearly stated, "In any criminal prosecution brought by the United States . . . a confession . . . shall

"CITE MIRANDA AND GO FREE"

Journalist James J. Kilpatrick of the *Sarasota Journal* reported immediately on Congress's passing of the Omnibus Crime Act. In an article titled "Cite Miranda and Go Free," he wrote,

> The United States Senate last week dealt the Supreme Court the strongest rebuke that has been officially hurled at the court in more than 30 years. . . . The Senate has said bluntly that it wants to see a balance restored between the rights of a defendant and the rights of society. The step is long overdue.[16]

Kilpatrick boldly called supporters of *Miranda* "knee-jerk liberals who bleed for the rights of rapists."[17]

In the late 1960s, many Americans, including President Johnson, blamed the rise in crime on the Supreme Court's *Miranda* ruling.

be admissible in evidence if it is voluntarily given."[18]
It went on to state that it was up to the trial judge
to determine if a statement was voluntary and could
be used in the trial. The law essentially overturned
Miranda on the federal level; lawmakers hoped the states
would follow the example of the federal courts as they
often did.

Nixon on *Miranda*

In the following
month, July 1968,
candidates running
for president of the
United States hit
the campaign trails.
Richard Nixon's
platform was the
nation's increasing
crime rate. He
blamed President

> " I have great respect
> for the Supreme
> Court. . . . But the Supreme Court
> is not infallible. It is sometimes
> wrong. Many of its decisions
> break down 5–4, and I think that
> often in recent years, the five man
> majority has been wrong, and the
> four man minority has been
> right."[19]
>
> —*RICHARD NIXON, IN A CAMPAIGN
> SPEECH*

Johnson; he blamed Attorney General William Ramsey
Clark; and primarily, he blamed the US Supreme Court
for its *Miranda* ruling. He promised to restructure
the court and strengthen the forces against crime. In a
campaign speech, he said, "the duty of a Justice of the

As a presidential candidate, Richard Nixon was vocal in his condemnation of the *Miranda* decision.

A NEW CHIEF JUSTICE OF THE SUPREME COURT

In 1968, Chief Justice Earl Warren retired from the US Supreme Court. He served another term, however, until an acceptable successor was appointed. In 1969, President Nixon appointed a successor—Warren E. Burger, the outspoken judge who vehemently opposed Chief Justice Warren and his *Miranda* decision. Nixon had promised Americans in his campaign that he would appoint a chief justice to the US Supreme Court who held to a strict interpretation of the US Constitution.

US Supreme Court is to interpret the law and not to make the law."[20]

In November 1968, Nixon was elected president of the United States. Chief Justice Warren had announced his retirement in 1968, which allowed Nixon to appoint a new chief justice: *Miranda* critic Warren Burger. He was confirmed by the senate and sworn in as chief justice in June 1969. During the first week of the new session, which started in October, the justices met in private to decide which petitions for writs of certiorari they would grant. Several hundred petitions had been filed over the summer of 1969 and hundreds more were held over from the previous term. It was a new era for the Supreme Court and for the

United States; however, the effects of *Miranda* would continue to linger in law enforcement agencies throughout the country. ～

Warren Burger took over as chief justice of the Supreme Court in 1969. He was much more conservative than his predecessor, Earl Warren.

Chapter 9

Law Enforcement Adjusts

*I*n the nearly half century since the *Miranda* ruling, the nature of police interrogations has changed profoundly. Police found new ways to conduct investigations, revised their training manuals, and retrained personnel. They found other ways to question suspects and subtle ways to get around *Miranda*. Law enforcement adapted to the restrictions of the Supreme Court decision and, as a result, often improved their interrogation practices.

More Structured Arrests

Following the *Miranda* decision, law enforcement developed procedures that generally would pass the

Miranda test if confessions were challenged in court. It became automatic for a police officer to read the Miranda warning to a suspect being taken into custody. The warning usually came right after an official arrest and before an interrogation.

When an interrogation or confession was being recorded, police made sure the Miranda warning was given at the beginning. The suspect had to verbally waive his or her rights in order for the interrogation to continue. The recording was often important evidence at trial to prove a police investigator had, in fact, given a suspect in custody his or her Miranda warning before the questioning began and before a confession was made.

The accused was also given the opportunity to have an attorney present. If a custodial suspect wanted an attorney but could not afford one, the state or federal government would provide an attorney. Questioning stopped until one was appointed. Usually, a list of available criminal defense attorneys was provided to police departments by the local bar association.

Before the *Miranda* decision, law enforcement officers might use intimidation methods or the third degree to get a suspect to confess. After *Miranda*, officers changed their strategies.

From Physical to Psychological

As time went on, interrogation procedures became more sophisticated. The Supreme Court had specifically mentioned interrogations in its opinion:

> *Even without employing brutality [or] the "third degree," . . . the very fact of custodial interrogation*

exacts a heavy toll on individual liberty, and trades on the weakness of individuals.[1]

Questioning in interrogation rooms shifted to a psychological approach, and the third degree essentially disappeared. Interrogators were trained to "project a sympathetic, friendly, and compassionate personality image."[2] Interrogators tried to earn the suspect's trust. The reason for the friendliness was obvious: "The interrogator firmly, relentlessly, and systematically implores the suspect to confess."[3]

Police officers were taught different techniques to work around the Miranda warnings. Officers relied on persuasion and occasionally misleading suspects to convince them to waive their Miranda rights. The

THE NONACCUSATORY INTERVIEW

In the 1970s, hundreds of thousands of private investigators, law enforcement officers, and federal government employees attended seminars on interrogation. They learned a technique designed to "persuade a guilty suspect to tell the truth but not so powerful as to cause an innocent person to confess."[4] This technique taught how to portray "an understanding and compassionate demeanor toward the suspect which allows the suspect to feel better about himself and the crime he committed."[5]

Supreme Court did not have a clear ruling regarding what a suspect could be told before being read the Miranda rights. Interrogators took advantage of this loophole by using softening-up tactics before giving a Miranda warning. Many of the tactics came from new police manuals teaching the art of police interrogation. They focused on convincing suspects to waive their rights or detailing the evidence against a suspect, implying the suspect was already known to be guilty. Interrogations included promises of leniency after lengthy questioning behind closed doors. Suspects were often convinced that confessing was good for their conscience, good for their families, and good for society as a whole. The following excerpts are from one interrogation, cited in the US Court of Appeals case *Miller v. Fenton*, which eventually made it to the Supreme Court:

> *INTERROGATOR. I don't think you're a criminal, Frank.*
>
> *SUSPECT FRANK MILLER. No, but you're trying to make me one.*
>
> *INTERROGATOR. No I'm not, no I'm not, but I want you to talk to me so we can get this thing worked out. . . . I'm on your side, Frank. I'm your brother,*

you and I are brothers, Frank. We are brothers, and I want to help my brother. . . . You killed this girl, didn't you?

MILLER. *No, I didn't.*

INTERROGATOR. *Honest, Frank? . . . you've got to help yourself before anybody else can help you. And we're going to see to it that you get the proper help. This is our job, Frank. This is our job. This is what I want to do.*[6]

The Reid Technique

The most well-known police-training manual, *Criminal Interrogation and Confessions*, was written in 1962 by Fred Inbau and John Reid. The US Supreme Court cited and directly quoted the manual in its *Miranda* opinion as an example of menacing interrogation practices that violated an individual's constitutional rights. In 1967,

THE COURT AND THE REID TECHNIQUE

In 1994, the US Supreme Court, in *Stansbury v. California*, referred to *Criminal Interrogation and Confessions* by Inbau, Reid, Buckley, and Jayne. In 2004, the court included a positive reference to the criminal interrogation methods of the Reid Technique in its *Missouri v. Seibert* opinion.

one year after the *Miranda* decision, Inbau and Reid revised their manual to incorporate the requirements of *Miranda*.

The Reid technique, as it came to be called, became the foundation for training police officers in interrogation techniques to elicit confessions. It was a step-by-step guide to simple psychological principles of questioning. As law enforcement changed through the years, the manual was revised again and again.

Skirting *Miranda*

One of the main concerns after *Miranda* was that more and more criminals would go free. Police officers feared conviction rates would plummet. After 1966, law enforcement sought ways to skirt the *Miranda* requirements. Sometimes a law enforcement officer would opt against questioning a suspect who was likely to use *Miranda* on appeal. In those cases, officers looked for other evidence to prove a suspect was guilty.

Since the *Miranda* rules applied only to suspects who were in custody, police shifted to casual interviews at the scene of a crime or scheduled interviews at a neutral location. Most interviews began before someone was placed under arrest. Although these types of

DAVIS V. UNITED STATES

In 1994, the US Supreme Court ruled on *Davis v. United States*, which significantly weakened *Miranda*. Davis, a member of the US Navy, was charged with murder. In his first interrogation, he waived his right to remain silent and his right to counsel.

The Supreme Court opinion described the events that took place:

> *About an hour and a half into the interview, he said, "Maybe I should talk to a lawyer." However, when the agents inquired if he was asking for a lawyer, he replied that he was not. They took a short break, he was reminded of his rights, and the interview continued for another hour, until he asked to have a lawyer present before saying anything more.*[7]

At trial, Davis asked that his statements during the interview not be allowed into evidence. A military judge denied his request. The judge held that Davis's "*mention* of a lawyer during the interrogation was not a request for counsel."[8] David was convicted of murder. A court of military appeals and the US Supreme Court upheld his conviction. The Supreme Court ruled a suspect must be explicit in his or her requests for a lawyer, and police are not required to follow up on vague requests for counsel.

interviews were not as successful as interrogation-room questioning, they were better than no interviews at all.

In 1983, law enforcement officers received help from the Supreme Court case *California v. Beheler*. Jerry Beheler, a suspect in a homicide, rode to the police station with police officers who told him he was not under arrest. Police officers did not read him his Miranda rights. After interviewing him for less than 30 minutes, Beheler admitted to being present when the crime occurred and left. Five days later, police arrested him. This time, they read him his Miranda rights and Beheler confessed. At trial, both statements were entered into evidence, and Beheler was convicted of murder.

> " Miranda warnings are not required simply because the questioning takes place in a coercive environment in the station house or because the questioned person is one whom the police suspect."[10]
>
> —US SUPREME COURT OPINION, CALIFORNIA V. BEHELER

In Beheler's first appeal, the California appellate court reversed his conviction, ruling that he should have been Mirandized before his first interview. The US Supreme Court ruled otherwise. On July 6, 1983, the court stated the Miranda warning was not required at the first interview because Beheler "was neither taken into custody for the first interview nor significantly deprived of his freedom of action."[9]

Beheler gave police what they needed to interview and interrogate suspects more freely before an arrest was made. *Beheler* helped them avoid the risk of violating *Miranda*. Other cases softened and weakened the effects of *Miranda*. Over time, *Miranda* would erode, although the US Supreme Court would not get rid of it entirely. ~

Chapter 10

The Future for *Miranda* *v. Arizona*

$\mathcal{A}$lthough the effects of *Miranda* have weakened, reading Miranda rights to a suspect is still a common occurrence. Police, suspects, and much of the general population can recite the five rights almost word for word. Miranda warnings are heard repeatedly on television and in films; it has become routine for suspects to expect and sometimes waive those rights.

According to several studies, between 78 percent and 96 percent of suspects knowingly or unknowingly waive their Miranda rights.[1] As early as 1986, one

Most custodial suspects waive their Miranda rights, though there is a strong correlation between waiving of rights and innocence.

attorney noted "next to the warning label on cigarette packs, *Miranda* is the most widely ignored piece of official advice in our society."[2] In 2008, law Professor Charles Weisselberg evaluated *Miranda* through the years:

> *Miranda's contemporary impact thus appears rather limited. . . . Police, prosecutors, and courts have all adapted to and diluted Miranda, using it to advance their own objections rather than to enforce the privilege against self-incrimination or the right to counsel. . . . Rather than eliminating compulsion inside the interrogation room, it has motivated police to develop more subtle and sophisticated interrogation strategies.*[3]

Opponents and supporters of *Miranda* ask how such an explicit Supreme Court decision became so diluted and nearly ineffective. The answer lies in the US Supreme Court itself.

Case after Case

As always, the justices of the Supreme Court changed. Within ten years of *Miranda*, four of the five justices who were part of the majority decision were no longer with the court. Along with Chief Justice Warren, Justices

The Miranda warnings are common on movies and television shows such as *Law and Order*. Interrogators are often able to get around *Miranda* to elicit a confession.

UNITED STATES V. PETERSON

In the 2005 Supreme Court case *United States v. Peterson*, police took 50 minutes to tell suspect Larry D. Peterson what evidence they had against him. Then they administered his Miranda rights, obtained his waiver, and got him to confess. The Supreme Court ruled Peterson's rights had not been violated.

Fortas, Black, and Douglas had resigned or retired and been replaced. From 1969 through 1977, Republican presidents Richard Nixon and Gerald Ford appointed more conservative justices, and the liberal Warren court became the more conservative Burger court. Two consecutive conservative courts led by Chief Justice William Rehnquist and Chief Justice John Roberts followed the Burger court.

Throughout the years, the Supreme Court has not openly ruled against *Miranda*. In the decade following the initial ruling, the court was hesitant to accept petitions for writs of certiorari involving Miranda rights. From 1973 to 1977, petitions claiming Miranda rights were violated were filed by 35 defendants. The court agreed to hear only one of those cases. Individual cases have chipped away at *Miranda*'s strength and effectiveness—although no Supreme Court decision has completely eradicated *Miranda*. Other case rulings have reinforced *Miranda*'s importance. Repeatedly, the US Supreme Court has made exceptions to *Miranda*. On June 12, 1984, the court ruled in *New York v. Quarles* that a statement made without a Miranda warning can be used at trial if the public's safety is at risk. Other cases provided other exceptions.

Dickerson v. United States

In *Dickerson v. United States*, Charles Dickerson claimed he had not received his Miranda warning before making statements about his role in a series of armed bank robberies. On June 26, 2000, the US Supreme Court struck down Congress's Omnibus Crime Control Act of 1968—that a statement is admissible if it was made

THE INNOCENCE PROJECT

One of the basic principles of *Miranda v. Arizona* is to protect individuals from making self-incriminating statements or coerced confessions. In numerous trials, innocent people have been convicted based on false confessions. The Innocence Project was founded in 1992 to "assist prisoners who could be proven innocent through DNA testing."[4] The organization maintains that many wrongful convictions need to be overturned, and many innocent people need to be released from prison.

voluntarily. In the *Dickerson* opinion, the US Supreme Court held that "*Miranda*, being a constitutional decision of this Court, may not be in effect overruled by an Act of Congress."[5]

Missouri v. Seibert

On June 28, 2004, the Supreme Court announced another ruling affecting *Miranda*. In *Missouri v. Seibert*, Patrice Seibert was charged with conspiring to cover up the death of a mentally ill, 18-year-old man living with the family. He was left to die in the family's burning mobile home. Five days after the fire, police arrested Seibert but did not read her the Miranda rights. After an approximately 40-minute interrogation, Seibert confessed. After a 20-minute break, she received her Miranda warning and signed a waiver of her rights. The officer had her repeat her confession.

At trial, Seibert's attorney made a **motion** to suppress both confessions. The judge did not allow the first confession but admitted the second into evidence. Seibert was convicted of murder. In a 5–4 decision, the

motion—A formal proposal to a court or judge asking for an order, ruling, or direction.

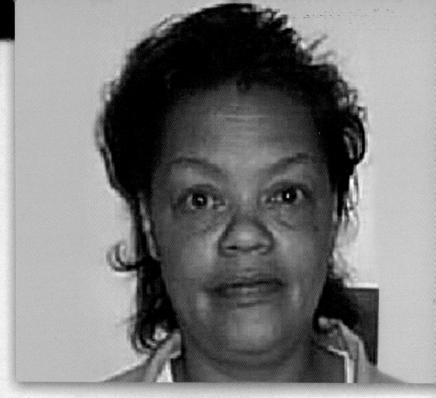

Patrice Seibert, 2003

US Supreme Court ruled that the second confession
was not admissible because the officer had intentionally
not given the Miranda warning to obtain it. However,
the evidence might have been admissible if the suspect
been given a longer break or informed that her initial
confession could not be used against her at trial.

Berghuis v. Thompkins

Six years later, the US Supreme Court heard oral
arguments on *Berghuis v. Thompkins*. The case was

a question of whether the suspect, Thompkins, had actually waived his Miranda rights. Police had advised Thompkins of his Miranda rights before questioning him about a shooting in which one person died. The court's opinion gave the details of what happened next:

> At no point did Thompkins say that he wanted to remain silent, that he did not want to talk with the police, or that he wanted an attorney. He was largely silent during the 3-hour interrogation, but near the end, he answered "yes" when asked if he prayed to God to forgive him for the shooting.[6]

> "Thompkins' silence during the interrogation did not invoke his right to remain silent. . . . Had Thompkins said that he wanted to remain silent or that he did not want to talk, he would have invoked his right to end the questioning. He did neither."[7]
>
> —US SUPREME COURT OPINION, BERGHUIS V. THOMPKINS

Thompkins asked the trial court to suppress his confession—the simple word *yes*—because his three hours of silence implied that he had not waived his right to remain silent. The judge denied the request. The jury

WARNING AS TO YOUR RIGHTS

You are under arrest. Before we ask you any questions, you must understand what your rights are.

You have the right to remain silent. You are not required to say anything to us at any time or to answer any questions. Anything you say can be used against you in court.

You have the right to talk to a lawyer for advice before we question you and to have him with you during questioning.

If you cannot afford a lawyer and want one, a lawyer will be provided for you.

If you want to answer questions now without a lawyer present you will still have the right to stop answering at any time. You also have the right to stop answering at any time until you talk to a lawyer.   P-4475

Even though the *Miranda* ruling has been weakened over time, the Miranda warnings are still recited to suspects as they are taken into police custody.

found Thompkins guilty; he was sentenced to life in prison without parole.

On June 1, 2010, the US Supreme Court voted 5–4 to uphold the trial court's verdict. It was the court's opinion that a suspect must clearly state he is exercising his Miranda rights. By speaking, the court ruled the suspect had waived his right to remain silent, even though he had not explicitly said so. It also established

VIDEOTAPED INTERROGATIONS

Given *Miranda*'s failures, some people wonder how a suspect's constitutional rights can be salvaged. One suggestion is to require interrogations to be videotaped. Some states, such as Alaska and Minnesota, already have that requirement. Other states require interrogations to be videotaped only under certain circumstances. In 2006, the Utah State Bar Association urged the Utah Supreme Court to make videotaping of interrogations mandatory. It reasoned,

> *With the simple flip of a switch, the courts can be provided with a record of everything that transpires during a custodial interrogation. Recording is a reasonable safeguard, which will ensure the protection of an accused's right to counsel, right against self-incrimination, and his or her right to a fair trial. Recording will also protect law enforcement from false claims of coercion and improper conduct.*[8]

the distinction that while suspects have the right to remain silent, they must clearly assert this right or their right to counsel. If a suspect does not assert these rights, the questioning can legally continue.

The Future of *Miranda*

In nearly half a century since the *Miranda* decision, the US Supreme Court has ruled on many cases involving

Miranda rights. The court has upheld the basic principle of *Miranda*, but it has weakened its strict nature little by little.

Supporters of the 1966 *Miranda v. Arizona* decision believe the US Supreme Court is turning back the clock on constitutional rights for the accused. They believe the court's decisions allow citizens to be too easily misled or intimidated into confessions. Most of all, they believe citizens are being denied their rights under the Fifth, Sixth, and Fourteenth amendments to the US Constitution

Opponents of *Miranda* support the US Supreme Court as it chips away at the Supreme Court case they have always disdained. No matter what happens with *Miranda* in the coming years, it can be seen as a monumental decision that brought the importance of informing suspects of their constitutional rights to the forefront of Americans minds. ～

TIMELINE OF EVENTS AND RULINGS

| 1791 | December 15 | The Bill of Rights becomes the first ten amendments to the US Constitution. |

| 1868 | July 9 | The Fourteenth Amendment to the US Constitution is passed. |

| 1932 | November 7 | The US Supreme Court reverses the lower court's decision in *Powell v. Alabama,* ruling that in certain instances, federal defendants have a right to counsel. |

| 1938 | May 23 | The Supreme Court rules in *Johnson v. Zerbst* that if a federal defendant is poor, an attorney must be provided. |

| 1941 | March 9 | Ernesto Miranda is born in Mesa, Arizona. |

| 1963 | March 2–3 | Ernesto Miranda kidnaps and rapes 18-year-old "Jane Smith" in Phoenix, Arizona. |

| | March 18 | The US Supreme Court rules in *Gideon v. Wainwright* that counsel must be provided to an impoverished defendant in all criminal cases. |

| | June 27 | Miranda is sentenced to serve prison time for kidnapping and rape. |

| 1964 | June 22 | The Supreme Court rules in *Escobedo v. Illinois* that in certain circumstances a suspect has the right to an attorney when being interrogated by police. |

| 1965 | April 22 | The Arizona Supreme Court denies Miranda's appeal and upholds the lower court's convictions. |

1965	April 22	The Arizona Supreme Court denies Miranda's appeal and upholds the lower court's convictions.
	June	ACLU lawyers John Flynn and John Frank file Miranda's appeal pro bono.
	November 22	The Supreme Court votes to hear *Miranda v. Arizona*.
1966	February 28–March 1	The US Supreme Court hears oral arguments on *Miranda v. Arizona*.
	June 13	The US Supreme Court reverses Miranda's convictions, granting a retrial in the lower court.
1967	February 15–23	Miranda is tried and found guilty a second time in the Superior Court of Maricopa County.
1968	June 19	President Lyndon B. Johnson signs The Omnibus Crime Control and Safe Streets Act of 1968 into law.
1972	December	Miranda is granted parole and released from prison.
1976	January 31	Miranda is stabbed to death in a bar fight in downtown Phoenix, Arizona.
1983	July 6	The Supreme Court ruling on *California v. Beheler* weakens *Miranda*.
2000	June 26	The US Supreme Court strikes down the Omnibus Crime Control Act of 1968 as unconstitutional.
2010	June 1	The US Supreme Court upholds the confession obtained in *Berghuis v. Thompkins*, ruling that suspects must explicitly state they are exercising their Miranda rights during interrogations.

GLOSSARY

catalyst
> An agent that causes change.

coerced
> Forced to think or act in a certain way as a result of pressure, intimidation, threats, or force.

counsel
> A lawyer who advises a person on legal matters.

custody
> The state of being detained or held by police.

incriminate
> To imply or suggest guilt.

interrogation
> Questioning by police, prosecutors, or other law enforcement officials.

Mirandize
> To inform a suspect of his or her Miranda rights.

parole

The conditional early release of a prisoner who is then monitored to comply with certain conditions for a specific period of time.

penitentiary

A US state or federal prison.

perpetrator

One who causes or executes something, such as a crime.

plea bargain

An agreement with a prosecutor where a defendant agrees to plead guilty for a reduced penalty.

BRIEFS

Petitioner

Ernesto Miranda

Respondent

State of Arizona

Date of Ruling

June 13, 1966

Summary of Impacts

After being arrested for kidnapping and rape, Ernesto Miranda was interrogated by law enforcement officials of the Phoenix, Arizona, police department. He was not told he had the right to the assistance of counsel or that he did not have to make statements that would incriminate himself. As a result of the questioning, Miranda confessed to raping a young woman and was convicted. Through efforts of the American Civil Liberties Union, attorneys John Flynn and John Frank appealed Miranda's case to the US Supreme Court in 1965.

The court heard the case in 1966. On June 13, 1966, the US Supreme Court ruled on *Miranda v. Arizona*. The 5–4 ruling reversed Miranda's conviction. The majority opinion stated that police procedures must ensure an individual is given his or her constitutional rights under the Fifth Amendment to avoid self-incrimination when in police custody. The court's opinion spelled out the procedures that law enforcement officials must follow to guarantee a suspect's constitutional rights under the Fifth Amendment. The court emphasized that an individual must be informed of his or her right to remain silent and right to have an attorney present during an interrogation. These procedures came to be called the Miranda rights or Miranda warning. Although subsequent decisions of the US Supreme Court have weakened *Miranda v. Arizona*, the ruling still stands.

Quote

"I fought [the *Miranda* case] on technicalities of the law, constitutional grounds, protected every right he possibly had. . . . That's what he's entitled to. And that's exactly what a person who's accused is entitled to, whether he's guilty or whether he's innocent. . . . That's what our whole system is structured around."

—*John Flynn, defense lawyer for Ernesto Miranda*

ADDITIONAL RESOURCES

Selected Bibliography

Friedman, Barry. "The Wages of Stealth Overruling (with Particular Attention to Miranda v. Arizona)." *Georgetown Law Journal* 99.1 (2010). PDF file. Web. 6 March 2012.

Miranda v. Arizona. 384 US 436. Supreme Court of the US. 1966. *Cornell University Law School*. Legal Information Inst., n.d. Web. 21 July 2011.

Stuart, Gary L. *Miranda: The Story of America's Right to Remain Silent*. Tucson: U of Arizona P, 2004. Print.

Weisselberg, C. D. "Mourning *Miranda*." *California Law Review*. 96.6 (2008): 1519. Print.

Further Readings

Pederson, Charles E. *The U.S. Constitution and the Bill of Rights*. Edina, MN: Abdo, 2010. Print.

Stocks, Jeffrey D. *Supreme Court Decisions*. Waco, TX: Prufrock, 2008. Print.

Web Links

To learn more about *Miranda v. Arizona*, visit ABDO Publishing Company online at **www.abdopublishing.com**. Web sites about *Miranda* are featured on our Book Links page. These links are routinely monitored and updated to provide the most current information available.

Places to Visit

Arizona State Library, Archives and History Division
1901 West Madison, Phoenix, AZ 85009
602-926-3720
http://www.lib.az.us/archives/county_maricopa_court_
miranda.aspx
The Archives and History Division of the Arizona State
Library houses the original documents in the *State of Arizona v.
Miranda* case from 1963 to 1971.

Arizona State Prison, Florence
1305 East Butte Avenue, Florence, AZ 85132
520-868-4011
http://www.azcorrections.gov/prisons/Jeff_Florence.aspx
Arizona's main state prison located in Florence is where Ernesto
Miranda served time.

The Supreme Court of the United States
One First Street NE, Washington, DC 20543
202-479-3000
http://www.supremecourt.gov/
The Supreme Court Building, home of the US judicial branch
of government, is located in Washington DC. Lectures,
exhibitions, and a film are available for visitors.

SOURCE NOTES

Chapter 1. Waiting for an Answer

1. H. Mitchell Caldwell and Michael S. Lief. "You Have the Right to Remain Silent." *American Heritage* 57.4 (2006). Web. 29 June 2011.

2. Mark Gribben. "Miranda vs. Arizona: The Crime that Changed American Justice." *truTV*. Turner Entertainment Networks, Inc., n.d. Web. 12 July 2011.

3. H. Mitchell Caldwell, and Michael S. Lief. "You Have the Right to Remain Silent." *American Heritage* 57.4 (2006). Web. 29 June 2011.

4. Liva Baker. *Miranda: Crime, Law and Politics*. New York: Atheneum, 1983. Print. 13.

5. Ibid.13.

6. Ibid.13.

7. Arizona Supreme Court in State v. Miranda. 401 P.2d 721. Supreme Court of Arizona. 1965. *Law Library—American Law and Legal Informatio*n. Net Industries, n.d. Web. 13 Feb. 2012.

8. Ibid.

9. Ibid.

10. Ibid.

11. Ibid.

12. Ibid.

13. Liva Baker. *Miranda: Crime, Law and Politics*. New York: Atheneum, 1983. Print. 13.

14. Arizona Supreme Court in State v. Miranda. 401 P.2d 721. Supreme Court of Arizona. 1965. *Law Library—American Law and Legal Information.* Net Industries, n.d. Web. 13 Feb. 2012.

15. Ibid.

16. "An American Time Capsule: Three Centuries of Broadside and Other Print Ephemera." *American Memory.* Library of Congress, n.d. Web. 3 July 2011.

17. Liva Baker. *Miranda: Crime, Law and Politics*. New York: Atheneum, 1983. Print. 61.

Chapter 2. Rights of the Accused

1. "The Bill of Rights: A Brief History." *ACLU*. ACLU, 4 March 2002. Web. 27 July 2011.

2. Liva Baker. *Miranda: Crime, Law and Politics*. New York: Atheneum, 1983. Print. 67.

3. "14th Amendment to the Constitution Was Ratified July 28, 1868." *America's Story from America's Library*. The Library of Congress, n.d. Web. 7 July 2011.

4. "US Constitution: Fifth Amendment." *FindLaw for Legal Professionals*. FindLaw, n.d. Web. 16 July 2011.

5. Ibid.

6. "US Constitution: Sixth Amendment." *FindLaw for Legal Professionals*. FindLaw, n.d. Web. 16 July 2011.

7. "Wickersham Commission." *Law Library—American Law and Legal Information*. Net Industries, n.d. Web. 15 July 2011.

8. Ibid.

9. Powell v. Alabama. 287 US 46. Supreme Court of the US. 1932. *Justia.com*. Justia, n.d. Web. 7 July 2011.

10. Ibid.

11. Ibid.

12. Johnson v. Zerbst. 304 US 458. Supreme Court of the US. 1938. *FindLaw for Legal Professionals*. FindLaw, n.d. Web. 13 July 2011.

13. Ibid.

14. Betts v. Brady. 316 US 455. Supreme Court of the US. 1942. *Cornell University Law School*. Legal Information Inst., n.d. Web. 13 July 2011.

15. Gideon v. Wainwright. 372 US 335. Supreme Court of the US. 1963. *FindLaw for Legal Professionals*. FindLaw, n.d. Web. 13 July 2011.

16. Ibid.

17. "Petition for a Writ of Certiorari from Clarence Gideon to the Supreme Court of the United States, 06/05/1962." *The National Archives*. The US National Archives and Records Administration, 6 May 1962. Web. 15 July 2011.

Chapter 3. The Man and His Crimes

1. Arizona Supreme Court in State v. Miranda. 401 P.2d 721. Supreme Court of Arizona. 1965. *Law Library—American Law and Legal Information*. Net Industries, n.d. Web. July 2011.

SOURCE NOTES CONTINUED

2. Richard A. Leo, and George C. Thomas III. *The Miranda Debate: Law, Justice, and Policing.* York, PA: Maple Press, 1998. Print. 8.

3. Arizona Supreme Court in State v. Miranda. 401 P.2d 721. Supreme Court of Arizona. 1965. *Law Library—American Law and Legal Information.* Net Industries, n.d. Web. July 2011.

4. Mark Gribben. "Miranda vs. Arizona: The Crime that Changed American Justice." *truTV.* Turner Entertainment Networks, Inc., n.d. Web. 12 July 2011.

5. Arizona Supreme Court in State v. Miranda. 401 P.2d 721. Supreme Court of Arizona. 1965. *Law Library—American Law and Legal Information.* Net Industries, n.d. Web. July 2011.

6. Liva Baker. *Miranda: Crime, Law and Politics.* New York: Atheneum, 1983. Print. 9.

7. Mark Gribben. "Miranda vs. Arizona: The Crime that Changed American Justice." *truTV.* Turner Entertainment Networks, Inc., n.d. Web. 12 July 2011.

8. Liva Baker. *Miranda: Crime, Law and Politics.* New York: Atheneum, 1983. Print. 12.

9. Ibid. 12.

10. Mark Gribben. "Miranda vs. Arizona: The Crime that Changed American Justice." *truTV.* Turner Entertainment Networks, Inc., n.d. Web. 12 July 2011.

11. Liva Baker. *Miranda: Crime, Law and Politics.* New York: Atheneum, 1983. Print. 13.

Chapter 4. Trial and First Appeal

1. Liva Baker. *Miranda: Crime, Law and Politics.* New York: Atheneum, 1983. Print. 19.

2. Ibid. 23.

3. Mark Gribben. "Miranda vs. Arizona: The Crime that Changed American Justice." *truTV.* Web. 16 July 2011.

4. Ibid.

5. "Statistics." *Rape, Abuse & Incest National Network (RAINN).* RAINN, 2009. Web. 17 July 2011.

6. Gary L. Stuart. *Miranda: The Story of America's Right to Remain Silent.* Tucson: U of Arizona P, 2004. Print. 41.

7. Escobedo v. Illinois. 378 US 478. Supreme Court of US. 1964. *Law Library—American Law and Legal Information*. Net Industries, n.d. 16 July 2011.

8. Escobedo v. Illinois. 378 US 478. Supreme Court of US. 1964. *Law Library—American Law and Legal Information*. Net Industries, n.d. 16 July 2011.

9. Ibid.

10. Arizona Supreme Court in State v. Miranda. 401 P.2d 721. Supreme Court of Arizona. 1965. *Law Library—American Law and Legal Information*. Net Industries, n.d. Web. July 2011.

11. Arizona Supreme Court in State v. Miranda. 401 P.2d 721. Supreme Court of Arizona. 1965. *Law Library—American Law and Legal Information*. Net Industries, n.d. Web. July 2011.

12. Ibid.

13. Liva Baker. *Miranda: Crime, Law and Politics*. New York: Atheneum, 1983. Print. 34.

Chapter 5. Petitioning the US Supreme Court

1. Joan Rapczynski. "The Legacy of the Warren Court." *Yale-New Haven Teachers Institute*. Yale-New Haven Teachers Institute, 1 April 2007. Web. 18 July 2011.

2. "US Constitution: Fourteenth Amendment." *FindLaw for Legal Professionals*. FindLaw, n.d. Web. 18 July 2011.

3. Liva Baker. *Miranda: Crime, Law and Politics*. New York: Atheneum, 1983. Print. 63.

4. Ibid. 64.

5. "ABA Model Rule 6.1 Voluntary Pro Bono Publico Service." *American Bar Association*. ABA, n.d. Web. 22 July 2011.

6. Liva Baker. *Miranda: Crime, Law and Politics*. New York: Atheneum, 1983. Print. 84.

7. Miranda v. Arizona. 384 US 436. Supreme Court of US. 1966. *FindLaw for Legal Professionals*. FindLaw, n.d. Web. 6 March 2012.

8. Liva Baker. *Miranda: Crime, Law and Politics*. New York: Atheneum, 1983. Print. 83.

9. "The Court Building." *Supreme Court of the United States*. Supreme Court of the US, n.d. Web. 19 July 2011.

SOURCE NOTES CONTINUED

10. "Danny Escobedo: Apr. 29, 1966." *TIME Magazine*. TIME, n.d. Web. 19 July 2011.

Chapter 6. Landmark Decision

1. Liva Baker. *Miranda: Crime, Law and Politics*. New York: Atheneum, 1983. Print. 107.

2. Ibid. 107.

3. Mark Gribben. "Miranda vs. Arizona: The Crime that Changed American Justice." *truTV*. Web. 16 July 2011.

4. Liva Baker. *Miranda: Crime, Law and Politics*. New York: Atheneum, 1983. Print.109.

5. "About the ACLU." *American Civil Liberties Union*. ACLU, n.d. Web. 18 July 2011.

6. "Supreme Court History." *PBS Newshour*. MacNeil/Lehrer Productions, 1 Jan. 2003. Web. 4 July 2011.

7. "Miranda v. Arizona, Oral Argument." U of MN, 28 Feb. 1966. Web. 19 July 2011.

8. Ibid.

9. "Interrogation and Confession." *Law Library—American Law and Legal Information*. Net Industries, n.d. Web. 3 July 2011.

10. "Miranda v. Arizona, Oral Argument." U of MN, 28 Feb. 1966. Web. 19 July 2011.

11. Ibid.

12. Ibid.

13. Liva Baker. *Miranda: Crime, Law and Politics*. New York: Atheneum, 1983. Print. 139.

14. "Miranda v. Arizona, Oral Argument." U of MN, 28 Feb. 1966. Web. 19 July 2011.

15. Ibid.

16. Ibid.

17. *Miranda v. Arizona*. 384 US 436. Supreme Court of the US. 1966. *Cornell University Law School*. Legal Information Inst., n.d. Web. 21 July 2011.

18. Ibid.

Chapter 7. After the Ruling

1. *Miranda v. Arizona.* 384 US 436. Supreme Court of the US. 1966. *Cornell University Law School.* Legal Information Inst., n.d. Web. 21 July 2011.

2. Ibid.

3. Ibid.

4. Ibid.

5. Ibid.

6. Liva Baker. *Miranda: Crime, Law and Politics.* New York: Atheneum, 1983. Print. 192.

7. "Geiger Miranda Warning Card." *Chief.* Chief, n.d. Web. 21 July 2011.

8. *Miranda v. Arizona.* 384 US 436. Supreme Court of the US. 1966. *Cornell University Law School.* Legal Information Inst., n.d. Web. 21 July 2011.

9. Ibid.

10. Ibid.

11. "Fifth Amendment – Rights of Persons." *FindLaw for Legal Professionals.* FindLaw, n.d. Web. 22 July 2011.

12. Liva Baker. *Miranda: Crime, Law and Politics.* New York: Atheneum, 1983. Print. 192-193.

13. Ibid.193.

Chapter 8. Reactions to *Miranda v. Arizona*

1. Liva Baker. *Miranda: Crime, Law and Politics.* New York: Atheneum, 1983. Print. 177.

2. Lawrence S. Wrightsman and Mary L. Pitman. *The* Miranda *Ruling: Its Past, Present, and Future.* New York: Oxford UP, 2010. Print. 61.

3. Liva Baker. *Miranda: Crime, Law and Politics.* New York: Atheneum, 1983. Print. 205.

4. Ibid. 197.

5. Ibid. 195.

6. Lawrence S. Wrightsman and Mary L. Pitman. *The* Miranda *Ruling: Its Past, Present, and Future.* New York: Oxford UP, 2010. Print. 61.

7. Liva Baker. *Miranda: Crime, Law and Politics*. New York: Atheneum, 1983. Print. 195.

8. Miranda v. Arizona. 384 US 436. Supreme Court of the US. 1966. *Cornell University Law School*. Legal Information Inst., n.d. Web. 21 July 2011.

9. Ibid.

10. Lawrence S. Wrightsman and Mary L. Pitman. *The* Miranda *Ruling: Its Past, Present, and Future*. New York: Oxford UP, 2010. Print. 62.

11. Eric Longley. "The Miranda Warning." *St. James Encyclopedia of Pop Culture*. *BNET*. The CBS Interactive Business Network, 29 Jan 2002. Web. 23 July 2011.

12. Liva Baker. *Miranda: Crime, Law and Politics*. New York: Atheneum, 1983. Print. 200.

13. Ibid. 201.

14. Lyndon B. Johnson. "Special Message to the Congress on Crime and Law Enforcement." *The American Presidency Project*. Gerhard Peters—The American Presidency Project, 9 March 1966. Web. 25 July 2011.

15. Liva Baker. *Miranda: Crime, Law and Politics*. New York: Atheneum, 1983. Print. 207.

16. James J. Kilpatrick. "Cite Miranda and Go Free." *Sarasota Journal*. Google news, 24 May 1968. Web. 25 July 2011.

17. Ibid.

18. 18 USC. §3501. Admissibility of Confessions. *Cornell University Law School*. Legal Information Inst., n.d. Web. 25 July 2011.

19. Liva Baker. *Miranda: Crime, Law and Politics*. New York: Atheneum, 1983. Print. 245–246.

20. Ibid. 246.

Chapter 9. Law Enforcement Adjusts

1. Miranda v. Arizona. 384 US 436. Supreme Court of the US. 1966. *Cornell University Law School*. Legal Information Inst., n.d. Web. 21 July 2011.

2. Richard A. Leo and George C. Thomas III, Eds. *The Miranda Debate: Law, Justice, and Policing*. Boston: Northeastern University Press, 1998. Print. 66.

3. Ibid. 66.

4. Brian C. Jayne and Joseph P. Buckley. "The Reid Technique of Interrogation." *John E. Reid & Associates, Inc.* John E. Reid & Associates, Inc., 2004. Web. 26 July 2011.

5. Ibid.

6. Richard A. Leo and George C. Thomas III, Eds. *The Miranda Debate: Law, Justice, and Policing.* Boston: Northeastern UP, 1998. Print. 81.

7. Davis v. United States. 512 US 452. (1994). Supreme Court of the US. 1944. *Cornell University Law School.* Legal Information Inst., n.d. Web. 27 July 2011.

8. Ibid.

9. California v. Beheler. 463 US 1121. Supreme Court of the US. 1983. *Justia*.com. Justia, n.d. Web. 26 July 2011.

10. Ibid.

Chapter 10. The Future for *Miranda v. Arizona*

1. Lawrence S. Wrightsman and Mary L. Pitman. *The* Miranda *Ruling: Its Past, Present, and Future.* New York: Oxford UP, 2010. Print. 157.

2. Ibid. 157.

3. Ibid. 159.

4. "Mission Statement." *Innocence Project.* Innocence Project, n.d. Web. 27 July 2011.

5. Dickerson v. United States. 530 US 428. Supreme Court of the US. 2000. *Cornell University Law School.* Legal Information Inst., n.d. Web. 27 July 2011.

6. Berghuis v. Thompkins. 560 US ____. Supreme Court of the US. 2010. *Cornell University Law School.* Legal Information Inst., n.d. Web. 27 July 2011.

7. Ibid.

8. Walter F. Bugden, Jr., and Tara L. Isaacson. "Crimes, Truth and Videotape: Mandatory Recording of Interrogations at the Police Station." *Utah State Bar.* Utah State Bar, 30 Oct. 2006. Web. 27 July 2011.

INDEX

W

Y

About the Author

Sue Vander Hook is an independent writer from Mankato, Minnesota, with a master of arts in English from Minnesota State University. She currently teaches writing at two Minnesota colleges. She has written more than 30 educational books for children and young adults with an emphasis on major historical events and biographies of people who have made a difference. Her published works also include a high school curriculum and series on disease, technology, and sports.

About the Content Consultant

Yale Kamisar is Clarence Darrow Distinguished University Professor Emeritus of Law, University of Michigan, where he has taught for 39 years. He is author of *Police Interrogation and Confessions* (1980) and coauthor of all 12 editions of *Modern Criminal Procedure*, the most widely used law school casebook on criminal procedure. More than 20 of his books and articles have been quoted or cited by various justices of the US Supreme Court.